Why We Stop Thinking

Why We Stop Thinking

How Smart Tech Is Making Us Mentally Lazy

Rowan Hale

Mindful Pages

Published in 2025

ISBN: 9789371771917 (PB)
ISBN: 9789371773133 (eBook)

Published by

Mindful Pages
Imprint of Alpha Editions LLC
312 W. 2nd St #1834
Casper, WY 82601, USA

This book was developed using advanced writing tools to support the drafting and ideation process. All content has been thoughtfully curated, refined, and reviewed to ensure quality and relevance.

Content

Introduction
The High Cost of Low Friction

The modern world hums with a sleek efficiency. Tasks that once demanded attention, memory, or deliberation now unfold at a touch or a word. Phone numbers, directions, entertainment choices—these are offered pre-packaged, anticipating our needs before we even articulate them. What once required effort has become effortless; what once involved friction now flows seamlessly. Yet beneath this polished surface lies an undercurrent of loss—not of time, but of thought itself.

This book opens with a provocative premise: technologies designed to ease our cognitive load are excelling far beyond their promise. They are not merely tools of convenience; they are instruments subtly reshaping how we remember, pay attention, and process complexity. And critically, this transformation often occurs without our conscious consent.

We live in a celebrated era of access: information is abundant, connectivity is immediate, and artificial intelligence increasingly informs everyday decisions. Few would deny the benefits. But the quieter question—one rarely asked with seriousness—is this: what do we surrender when the act of thinking becomes optional?

The Unseen Trade

Technology has long been framed as liberatory. Tools extend our reach and amplify our capabilities. Yet tools also shape their users. A hammer encourages one mode of engagement, a telescope another. Smart technologies—those that anticipate, automate, and adapt—take this a step further: they remove the need to engage altogether. GPS systems render spatial reasoning optional. Predictive text pre-empts thought. Smart homes, digital assistants, curated feeds—these are cognitive prosthetics, outsourcing capacities once central to intellectual agility.

The seduction of these systems lies in subtlety. Unlike dystopian visions of overt control, the erosion of our faculties today is quiet, cumulative, and widely embraced. No alarms sound when our memory of city streets fades; no shock accompanies the next-word suggestion or personalised playlist. We interpret these intrusions as convenience. And yet, in these small, unremarkable moments, our patterns of attention, perception, and engagement are quietly rewired.

From Tool to Crutch

The core argument of *Why We Stop Thinking* is not that technology is inherently harmful. Rather, it is that the relentless pursuit of ease carries a hidden cost—a cost rarely accounted for. Tools intended to assist can, over time, become crutches. Habit transforms into default. As cognitive effort is increasingly outsourced, faculties that once defined human intelligence—memory, attention, judgment, spatial reasoning, narrative understanding, even curiosity—atrophy quietly, almost imperceptibly.

This is no Luddite nostalgia, no plea to return to paper maps or rotary phones. Nor is it a sensationalist warning of machines taking over. It is a subtler critique: that we willingly relinquish the very processes that make thinking distinctively human. And we do so not in crises, but in the comfort of daily routines.

Ease as a Value System

Convenience has become more than a feature—it has become a cultural ideal. Waiting, remembering, navigating, choosing—all are increasingly seen as inconveniences to be eliminated. Markets have responded decisively: every moment of friction is targeted for optimisation, every pause an opportunity for acceleration. Yet not all friction is undesirable. Much of what nurtures insight, creativity, and learning arises precisely from the effort that smooth design seeks to erase. Cognitive strain—the challenge of working through uncertainty, resisting distraction, persisting with difficulty—is not a flaw; it is the process itself.

This book asks a fundamental question: what happens when friction disappears entirely? When struggle is pre-empted, replaced by automation, the act of thinking is not lost, strictly speaking—but it is no longer demanded.

The Disappearing Mind

Research is beginning to confirm what intuition has long suggested. Reliance on GPS affects spatial memory. Constant digital interruptions diminish sustained attention, even offline. Externalising memory to search engines, reminders, and cloud storage reduces internalisation and retention. These are not incidental effects—they are structural, woven into the very design of the technologies we depend upon.

Even more concerning is the generational impact. Children growing up with predictive devices are not merely using different tools; they are developing distinct cognitive and behavioural patterns. Capacity for focus, patience, deep inquiry—these traits are cultivated through practice, not granted by default. And without engagement, they erode.

Reclaiming Agency in an Automated World

Where does this leave us? The book does not advocate wholesale disconnection or fear of technology. Its aim is subtler: to recognise, interrogate, and understand the patterns shaping our minds. Awareness, not abstinence, becomes the path forward. Engagement, not surrender, defines the goal.

Subsequent chapters examine the ways smart technologies shape discrete areas of cognition—navigation, memory, language, attention, decision-making, and more. They combine empirical science with cultural critique, tracing both the emergence of these tools and their quiet impact on thought. There is no alarmism here, only clarity: a careful account of what we surrender, often willingly, and what might yet be reclaimed.

The call to action is simple, though profound: think again. Rebuild the muscle of mental effort. Resist the drift toward passive cognition, not through fear, but through deliberate attention to the faculties that make us human. Tools shape us, yes—but so do our habits, our choices, and our willingness to engage with the world unsimplified.

We cannot—and need not—halt the advance of smart technology. Yet how we meet it matters. *Why We Stop Thinking* is an invitation to inhabit the present with awareness: to see, to question, and to remember what thinking, in its fullest sense, still entails.

Chapter 1
The Automation Reflex

The most profound shifts in human behaviour rarely arrive with a fanfare; they creep in quietly, disguised as convenience. A new device appears—efficient, helpful, almost imperceptible—and we welcome it. Not out of laziness, not out of inattention, but because it promises to save us from effort, from delay, from the ordinary frictions of daily life. And slowly, almost imperceptibly, it becomes part of the rhythm of our routines. Its presence goes unnoticed; its absence feels intolerable. We call this progress. Yet progress, when unexamined, carries a subtle reflex.

Increasingly, our world is structured around invisible aid—technologies designed not merely to assist, but to anticipate. Modern devices no longer wait for commands; they offer, predict, and complete. Email suggests your next sentence. Search engines finish your thought. Navigation systems reroute before you even realise you've strayed. Attention is bypassed. Outcomes are delivered without the involvement that once made them meaningful. Assistance has shifted from response to default. The machine does not ask if we want help; it assumes we do.

This is the automation reflex: a cultural and cognitive tendency where the path of least resistance becomes habitual. It is not merely a function of software, but a broader mindset, one in which effort is inefficiency and delay a flaw to be corrected. The ideal of the frictionless life quietly supplants the values of struggle, perseverance, and deliberate engagement. Philosophical as much as technological, this shift is only beginning to reveal its consequences.

To grasp how we arrived here, we must first consider the evolving meaning of convenience. In previous generations, convenience was a luxury—a welcome aid, not a replacement. The microwave, the automatic transmission, the answering machine: these simplified tasks without rendering the user obsolete. Convenience then augmented effort; it did not overwrite it. Today, that boundary has dissolved. Convenience acts pre-emptively, thinking ahead, relieving us of deciding, remembering, even noticing.

Consider scheduling a meeting. Once, it involved checking calendars, negotiating times, accommodating constraints—a small exercise of memory, communication, and patience. Now a digital assistant completes it in seconds. Or spelling a word: previously a pause to consider and recall; now the correct spelling materialises mid-thought. The outcome is achieved, yes—but the cognitive engagement, the subtle exertion of the mind, is bypassed. What was once a mental exercise becomes frictionless.

Automation is not inherently harmful; it is often profoundly useful. Its danger lies in ubiquity. When help is constant, it ceases to feel like help—it becomes expected. And when expectation goes unexamined, it transforms us—not only in what we do, but in how we think, and what we presume of ourselves.

Invisible help is insidious precisely because it is subtle. It does not confront autonomy with force; it erodes it through small, repeated handovers. A suggestion here, a completion there, a shortcut offered, accepted, then assumed. Over time, the line between tool and replacement blurs. We internalise the system; our own capacities recede. The device remembers, so we forget. The algorithm decides, so we defer. The machine thinks, so we relax.

Neuroscience captures some of these effects. Reliance on external assistance reshapes the brain—not dramatically, but noticeably. The prefrontal cortex, central to decision-making, shows reduced activation where outcomes are automated. Memory pathways weaken when recall is unnecessary. Attention networks fray under predictable conditions. The mind, like the body, responds to disuse with atrophy.

Behaviourally, the consequences are stark. With constant aid, tolerance for difficulty diminishes. Tasks once manageable now frustrate. Waiting becomes intolerable; complexity, aversive. Struggle is recast as inefficiency, rather than a sign of meaningful engagement. This is not laziness—it is habituation. The brain adapts to the easiest available pattern. In a world optimised for ease, that pattern often demands the least thinking.

Time, too, is reframed. Smart technology promises reclaimed hours, yet that time is often absorbed by the devices themselves. We check more emails, consume more content, juggle more notifications. The paradox is glaring: the more we 'save,' the less time feels meaningful. Automation fragments attention and dilutes presence. A calendar that schedules for us adds efficiency, but removes reflection. Predictive replies save keystrokes, but constrain intention. Step by step, our engagement shallows.

These transformations are systemic and accelerating. As AI embeds itself further into daily life, automation expands from routine to cognitive tasks. Machines mediate attention, filter perception, shape decisions. And because these interventions are invisible, they are hard to resist. You cannot question what you barely notice; you cannot resist a handover you are trained to accept.

This chapter examines the automation reflex: the uncritical acceptance of help, the conflation of ease with improvement, and the quiet surrender of cognitive space. We will trace how culture cultivates this reflex—how impatience with friction predisposes us to welcome smoothness, how our notions of efficiency and productivity have shifted from depth toward speed. Though gradual, these shifts are reshaping the terrain of thought itself.

We will interrogate invisible help—what it is, how it operates, and why it matters. We will explore convenience as a cultural imperative, its psychological and philosophical dimensions. We will observe how repeated assistance rewires expectation, alters behaviour, and reshapes attention. And we will challenge the assumption that time saved is automatically time gained, revealing how automation can hollow the experience of time itself.

This is not a call to abandon technology or retreat into nostalgia. It is an invitation to observe: to notice patterns long unexamined, to question defaults once accepted. To ask, with real curiosity: what is this relieving me from? And is that relief worth surrendering?

In the chapters ahead, we trace the automation reflex across cognition—from navigation and memory to communication and learning. It begins not with a sudden handover, but with gradual accommodation. Not with obvious loss, but with trade-offs. And like all trade-offs, it deserves scrutiny. For if we do not ask what we are giving up, we may one day find that we have surrendered far more than we intended—starting with the simple, yet profound, act of thinking for ourselves.

The Rise of Invisible Help

A device that finishes your sentence before you've formed it. A map that reorients the world for you before you realise you're lost. A news feed that adjusts your perspective by deciding what you see next. None of these tools demand our attention in an obvious way. They do not declare themselves as aids. They simply act. Quietly. Seamlessly. Efficiently. This is the defining characteristic of *invisible help*: it operates not by assisting you after a decision has been made, but by intervening before the need to decide arises at all.

Invisible help has become the signature gesture of smart design. It is elegant, frictionless, and often welcomed—especially in a world that prizes speed and minimal effort. But beneath its polished surface lies a deep philosophical transformation. Help, once associated with an active request or a specific need, has evolved into a default mode of interaction. Rather than responding to human intention, today's systems are designed to anticipate it—and in doing so, they often preclude it.

The shift is not merely technical; it is cognitive and cultural. It redefines what it means to act, to know, and to decide. When help becomes ambient—when it ceases to feel like assistance at all—it can quietly displace our capacity for engagement without setting off any mental alarms. We feel served, but not supplanted. And that feeling, while comforting, is also deceptive.

At the heart of this transformation is a simple idea: anticipation replaces initiation. Consider predictive text, one of the most widely used yet least examined features in modern communication. On the surface, it's a tool designed to speed up typing, reduce error, and enhance fluency. But its deeper effect lies in the way it subtly reorients authorship. You no longer reach for words; they arrive before your intent is fully formed. The decision is no longer between multiple conscious options, but between accepting a suggestion or resisting it. The technology proposes, and your role is reduced to consenting or correcting. This dynamic turns creation into curation—your thoughts edited before they're fully owned.

This anticipatory logic is spreading well beyond keyboards. Recommendation engines now shape the books we read, the shows we watch, the people we follow. Navigation apps redraw our mental maps in real time, not just telling us where to go but recalculating our route the moment we deviate. Smart thermostats adjust the temperature before we feel discomfort. Facial recognition systems unlock devices as we glance, removing even the need to remember. These are not simply tools that respond; they are systems that pre-empt.

The hallmark of invisible help is that it operates beneath the threshold of conscious awareness. It does not require our explicit consent because it rarely announces itself. We do not pause to evaluate whether we needed assistance; we experience the result as if it were natural. The machine intervenes without friction, and our own cognition recedes in kind. Effort that was once instructive becomes obsolete. In time, we forget the feel of it.

This bypassing of engagement has profound consequences for mental development. Psychologists have long understood that learning and memory are tightly linked to *effortful processing*—the mental exertion involved in encoding, retrieving, and manipulating information. When help becomes so seamless that it eliminates struggle altogether, we risk weakening the very processes that make knowledge durable. Cognitive psychologist Robert Bjork describes this phenomenon in terms of "desirable difficulty"—the idea that tasks which demand more mental effort often result in deeper learning and retention. Invisible help removes those difficulties, and with them, the benefits.

Moreover, the design logic behind invisible help is increasingly unaccountable. It is easy to forget that many of these anticipatory systems are governed not by neutral efficiency, but by underlying corporate incentives. A recommendation algorithm does not simply show you what you might like; it shows you what keeps you engaged—often by narrowing your exposure to the familiar or emotionally provocative. A navigation system does not always route you to the shortest path; it may steer traffic flow according to aggregated data or partnership agreements. Invisible help may appear user-centred, but it is often behaviourally manipulative.

This asymmetry of agency raises ethical questions. When systems anticipate your needs, they also define them. They influence what counts as a problem, what solutions are available, and whether you even realise a decision has occurred. Philosopher Michel Foucault warned that the most effective forms of power are those that shape the field of possible actions rather than impose overt constraints. Invisible help operates precisely in this register—not by denying choice, but by pre-empting it to such a degree that conscious choice becomes irrelevant.

It is important to understand that this transformation is not the result of malice or even bad design. It is the logical outcome of a design culture obsessed with frictionlessness. In the tech industry, "user friction" is treated as a flaw to be eliminated. Every extra tap, delay, or prompt is seen as a barrier to engagement. The result is a relentless drive toward systems that are intuitive, anticipatory, and ambient. But in the process, the user is gradually relieved of the very experiences—hesitation, deliberation, effort—that foster independent thinking.

The deeper danger lies in how these design choices recalibrate our expectations of the world. As more tasks are completed for us—without visible process or request—we become less tolerant of delay, error, and ambiguity. We expect systems to know before we tell them, to act before we ask. And when they don't, we grow impatient. In this way, invisible help reshapes not just how we engage with machines, but how we engage with life. Complexity becomes irritating. Uncertainty becomes unacceptable. The mental muscle built by navigating ambiguity atrophies, replaced by a reliance on systems that hide ambiguity altogether.

There are, of course, arguments in favour of such systems. Invisible help can enhance accessibility, reduce cognitive load, and free up attention for higher-order tasks. A surgeon relying on robotic assistance is not surrendering expertise but augmenting it. A visually impaired person using voice navigation is not bypassing thought but accessing it in a new modality. The problem is not help per se—it is the habituation to help without reflection. The issue is not that tools assist us, but that we no longer notice when, how, or why they do.

Invisible help becomes problematic not when it supports thinking, but when it displaces it. The difference is subtle, but consequential. Support invites engagement; displacement eliminates it. The moment a tool makes thought optional, it risks making thought unnatural. And when enough of our daily interactions are governed by such tools, we begin to encounter ourselves less often in our own actions.

A striking example of this dynamic can be found in the growing field of ambient intelligence—environments embedded with sensors, AI, and predictive systems that respond to behaviour automatically. In a smart home, lights dim as you relax, music adjusts to your mood, groceries are reordered without prompting. These features can enhance comfort, but they also remove the small frictions that once anchored us to our surroundings. We are no longer required to *notice* or *decide*—we simply receive. The house becomes responsive, but we become passive.

This passivity has a cost. Every time a task is completed for us without our involvement, we lose an opportunity for cognitive reinforcement. Over time, those losses accumulate—not dramatically, but incrementally. And because the process is gradual, we do not register it as decline. We interpret the absence of effort as progress, not realising that ease has quietly displaced understanding.

To resist this erosion, we must first learn to *see* invisible help—not to reject it wholesale, but to recognise its presence and evaluate its effect. This begins with noticing moments when our engagement is bypassed: when a thought is completed for us, when a choice is preselected, when a route is suggested before we recall the geography ourselves. It continues with asking whether the convenience offered is truly serving our goals—or merely training us to expect less of our own minds.

Invisible help is not a technological inevitability. It is a design decision, and one that can be questioned. We can ask for systems that support rather than replace human effort, that prompt reflection rather than eliminate it. We can value *transparency* over convenience, *participation* over prediction. And we can build a culture that does not equate help with absence of effort, but with the enhancement of engagement.

In the end, what is at stake is not our ability to use tools, but our willingness to remain active within them. The future of cognition will not be shaped by the tools themselves, but by the habits we form around them. Whether invisible help becomes a scaffold or a substitute depends on whether we choose to remain present in the process—or simply allow the process to act in our place.

Convenience as Culture

A society's defining values are often expressed not through its declarations, but through its defaults. One of the most quietly transformative shifts of the past half-century is the way *convenience* has moved from luxury to baseline. Where once ease was seen as a reward, today it is treated as a right. This evolution is not merely about comfort or efficiency—it represents a deeper reconfiguration of how we relate to effort, time, and even meaning itself. *Convenience has become a cultural expectation so pervasive that its absence now feels like a failure rather than a feature.* And with that expectation comes a profound consequence: a declining tolerance for friction, a shrinking appetite for delay, and an increasing estrangement from the cognitive exertion that underpins genuine learning, creativity, and resilience.

The language of modern product design offers an unambiguous window into this mindset. Terms like *frictionless, streamlined, intuitive,* and *one-click* are no longer mere selling points; they are imperatives. A product that demands effort, even minimal thought, is deemed poorly designed. A process that takes longer than a few seconds is considered broken. As behavioural scientist Nir Eyal notes, users are trained to abandon apps that do not deliver immediate gratification. The assumption is simple: convenience is not optional, and any interruption of it is a problem to be solved. That framing, repeated at scale across services, platforms, and daily routines, gradually reshapes our expectations—not only of technology, but of ourselves and one another.

It was not always this way. In mid-20th-century consumer culture, convenience was marketed as liberation—from domestic labour, from drudgery, from unnecessary complication. The microwave, the automatic washing machine, the pre-sliced loaf—each of these was framed as a marvel of modern life, an indication that progress was arriving in tangible, time-saving increments. Yet even then, convenience was still something to be noticed. It had novelty. It was named. To speak of a convenience food or a convenience store was to acknowledge that one was taking a shortcut. That language has faded. Today, to take the convenient route is not an exception—it is the default, often unconscious, choice. The very idea of a "shortcut" has lost its meaning when there is no longer a long route to compare it to.

This shift is not trivial. It alters how we interpret effort. The friction that once signalled meaningful engagement is now seen as inefficiency. Waiting, whether for a webpage to load or a response to a message, is no longer a natural part of the temporal fabric—it is a failure of optimisation. A map that requires us to orient ourselves, a recipe that asks for intuition rather than strict steps, a form that cannot autofill—these are interpreted not as invitations to engage, but as outdated or broken systems. *Convenience culture teaches us to resent anything that asks more of us than we've come to expect.*

One of the clearest expressions of this shift can be seen in the changing norms of digital communication. The rise of messaging apps and read receipts has eroded the social tolerance for delay. To be slow in responding is now, in many contexts, an unspoken breach of etiquette. A delayed reply is not simply a reflection of time constraints; it is interpreted as disregard, distraction, or disinterest. The cultural demand for immediacy reshapes the rhythm of conversation, pressuring individuals to respond before they've had time to reflect, to react instead of deliberate. Convenience, in this context, comes at the cost of depth.

This convenience reflex also alters our sense of agency. When systems are designed to remove barriers, they also remove opportunities to develop patience, skill, and discernment. Consider the evolution of photography. Taking and developing a photograph once required technical knowledge, physical handling, and a delay between capture and result. Today, we can take dozens of images in seconds, apply filters, and share them globally in less time than it once took to remove a lens cap. The democratization of photography has undoubtedly expanded creative access. But it has also changed the stakes. When effort drops to zero, so too can intentionality. Not always—but often enough to notice. *When everything is easy, nothing quite feels earned.*

Cognitive psychologist Daniel Kahneman's work on *System 1* and *System 2* thinking—fast, intuitive versus slow, effortful cognition—offers a useful framework here. Our preference for convenience plays directly to System 1, rewarding speed and ease while discouraging the kind of deliberate, analytical thinking that requires time and discomfort. This isn't merely a matter of preference. It is a neurological tendency reinforced by environmental design. When every system around us is optimised to reduce cognitive demand, we are less frequently invited into System 2 thinking. Over time, *the muscle of deep thought weakens from disuse.*

Culturally, this shift aligns with a broader pattern: the erosion of tolerance for what might be called "productive difficulty." Tasks that once required navigation, interpretation, or troubleshooting now arrive in pre-resolved formats. Music is no longer discovered through crate-digging or social recommendation, but through algorithmic suggestions tuned to our habits. News is delivered via personalised feeds designed to match our interests and preconceptions. Routes are calculated. Words are suggested. Purchases are pre-selected. There is a kind of intelligence behind all of it—but it is not ours. It is ambient, predictive, and often invisible. *The result is a paradoxical narrowing of experience in the name of individual choice.*

Of course, convenience has real value. It frees attention. It expands access. It reduces the cognitive load of menial or repetitive tasks. The problem arises when convenience is no longer one value among many, but the dominant value against which all others are judged. A convenience-first culture doesn't merely streamline tasks; it reconfigures what we consider worth doing at all. If a process cannot be simplified, is it worth engaging in? If a thought cannot be completed quickly, is it worth pursuing? These are the quiet calculations that convenience culture embeds in the background of our thinking.

This recalibration also affects how we consume information. As reading habits migrate from longform to scrollable, the design of content increasingly prioritises speed over substance. Platforms reward immediacy—headlines, summaries, soundbites—while discouraging complexity. Readers, in turn, begin to expect smoothness. A challenging sentence is now a stumbling block, not an invitation. A nuanced argument feels cumbersome. *Convenience in consumption breeds impatience in comprehension.*

The implications extend beyond the individual. When cultural systems reward efficiency over engagement, even institutions reorient themselves. Educational technologies are increasingly assessed by how quickly they deliver results, rather than how deeply they cultivate understanding. User experience in healthcare is often benchmarked against convenience metrics—waiting times, digital scheduling—rather than quality of interaction. Even politics, mediated through platforms designed for immediacy, is now shaped more by emotional speed than deliberative substance.

It is easy to miss the cumulative effect of these shifts, because each is presented as an upgrade, a solution to a minor annoyance. But culture is not made of grand gestures—it is shaped by a thousand microdecisions repeated until they form expectation. And when an entire society begins to expect that everything be fast, easy, and responsive, it also begins to lose patience with slowness, with ambiguity, and with the kind of difficulty that leads to mastery.

There is also a psychological cost to the universalisation of convenience: the erosion of *frustration tolerance*. The capacity to persist through discomfort, to delay gratification, to work through problems without immediate reward—these are foundational traits of mature cognition. They are also increasingly rare. Clinical psychologists have noted a rise in what some refer to as *distress intolerance*—a diminished ability to cope with even minor challenges without emotional disruption. While the causes are complex, the omnipresence of convenience is undoubtedly a contributing factor. When everything is engineered to go smoothly, the occasional bump can feel like a crisis.

Yet this is not a call to reject convenience wholesale. The point is not to idealise struggle for its own sake, but to recognise that effort is not the enemy of progress—it is often its engine. When we smooth every surface, we may also remove the texture that makes thought, discovery, and resilience possible. *A culture that never asks us to work for anything also fails to teach us what work is for.*

To move forward, we must begin to revalue friction—not as an obstacle, but as a meaningful part of experience. The act of learning something slowly, of writing something from scratch, of orienting oneself in an unfamiliar environment—these are not inefficient relics of the past. They are opportunities to reclaim a deeper form of presence. Not everything should be easy. Some things should be earned. Some processes should be opaque, demanding, even frustrating—not because that makes them noble, but because it makes them *real*.

If we can recover a tolerance for effort—not as a threat to convenience, but as a complement to it—we may begin to repair what has quietly thinned in the smoothness of our systems. Because convenience, when unexamined, not only shapes what we do. It shapes *who we become while doing it.* And what we become, over time, is a society less capable of staying with hard problems, less skilled in the art of self-direction, and less willing to inhabit the full span of our mental capacities. The tools we've built to save us time must not be allowed to steal our attention, or our agency. Convenience is a tool. Culture is a choice.

When Help Becomes Habit

Few transformations are as cognitively consequential—and as culturally invisible—as the process through which occasional help becomes habitual reliance. What begins as a convenience often ends as a dependency, not through coercion or compulsion, but through repetition and comfort. Help, in its modern form, is rarely dramatic. It is subtle, ambient, and increasingly automatic. Yet its cumulative effects are neither benign nor neutral. *Frequent assistance, especially when unexamined, changes not just what we do but how we are wired to think.* Over time, our mental architecture adapts not for resilience, but for outsourcing. The brain conserves what it no longer needs to use. And when we are persistently helped, we learn—at a neurocognitive level—to stop helping ourselves.

The relationship between dependence and assistance has long been studied in behavioural psychology. But what is different today is the scale and speed of technological help, and the fact that it increasingly intervenes before the user has even made a decision. Smart systems now predict, suggest, remind, correct, and execute—frequently without explicit input. This is no longer merely support; it is substitution. And substitution, once habitual, leads to behavioural deactivation. Consider the case of GPS-based navigation. Once regarded as a marvel of mobile technology, it has now become so embedded in the driving experience that many users report feeling disoriented in familiar areas when GPS is unavailable. Studies conducted at University College London have shown that regular use of digital navigation suppresses activation in the hippocampus—the region of the brain associated with spatial memory and wayfinding. *When we are consistently guided, we gradually lose our internal maps.*

This phenomenon is not confined to physical orientation. It extends across all domains where cognitive effort was once required and is now pre-empted by technology. Digital calendars and scheduling assistants mean we no longer need to remember appointments or rehearse future events in our minds. Predictive text tools offer vocabulary before we fully articulate intention. Content recommendations determine what we might want before we know we're looking. What these systems have in common is that they function as *externalised cognition*. They operate as mental surrogates, reducing the need for active recall, decision-making, and sometimes even curiosity. The reward, of course, is efficiency. But the cost is a decline in the cognitive engagement that once accompanied these tasks.

Neuroscience has a name for this pattern: *neuroplastic adaptation through disuse*. The brain, like any organ, adapts according to input. The circuits that are activated regularly strengthen through myelination and synaptic reinforcement. Those left dormant, by contrast, weaken. Cognitive functions such as working memory, problem-solving, and sustained attention are particularly vulnerable to underuse. When assistance becomes habitual, the user stops calling upon these circuits with the same intensity or frequency. The result is not an immediate deficit, but a gradual erosion of capacity. *The less we need to think, the less we become able to think.*

This shift is reinforced behaviourally through what psychologists term *learned passivity*. Originally studied in the context of trauma, the concept refers to the way individuals begin to internalise a sense of helplessness when effort consistently fails to produce agency. In the context of technology, the inverse is often true—assistance is so frictionless and rewarding that users begin to internalise the absence of effort as preferable. But the psychological result is strikingly similar: *a reduced impulse to initiate independent action*. If help is always one tap away—or, increasingly, one step ahead—why engage your own faculties at all?

Real-world behaviours mirror this shift. University students report lower motivation to memorise material when lecture slides and digital summaries are guaranteed. Office workers increasingly rely on auto-replies and templates to avoid crafting original messages. Parents use smart speakers to answer their children's questions rather than encouraging exploration or discussion. These are not failures of character; they are the predictable outcomes of environments that reward ease and discourage mental exertion. Over time, users begin to default not to their own capacities, but to the systems that stand ready to assist.

This rewiring is not only neurological or behavioural—it is also deeply cultural. As discussed in earlier sections, the expectation of convenience has become normative. To struggle with a task now signals, in many contexts, a lack of modernity. A person who forgets an appointment is not just seen as disorganised—they are seen as failing to use the tools properly. This inversion of expectation reinforces the dependence loop. When assistance becomes the standard, effort becomes an anomaly. And anomalies are often corrected, not explored.

There is, however, an important tension worth exploring. Not all help leads to dependency. Under the right conditions, assistance can be empowering—scaffolding that strengthens rather than supplants. The difference lies in *timing and intent*. Assistance that arrives *after* engagement—that supports a process already underway—tends to reinforce autonomy. For example, a tutor who helps a student after they've attempted a problem is reinforcing learning through feedback. A digital dictionary that is consulted after a reading attempt supports vocabulary development. In contrast, assistance that arrives *before* or *instead* of engagement risks becoming a substitute rather than a support. The key distinction is whether the user is participating in the process or merely receiving the output.

Design culture plays a critical role here. The most dependency-inducing systems are those designed to eliminate user effort entirely. This is often celebrated as innovation. But innovation that removes human agency from the equation must be scrutinised. A smart fridge that orders groceries without permission, a car that adjusts its path without explanation, a health app that interprets symptoms without fostering understanding—these are systems that may offer convenience but do so at the cost of cognitive presence. They train users to outsource not just action, but thought.

Importantly, this habituation is self-reinforcing. Once users grow accustomed to help, they not only expect it—they resist its absence. This is the behavioural equivalent of muscle atrophy: tasks that were once manageable now feel onerous. Users avoid friction not because it is unbearable, but because it is unfamiliar. The convenience threshold ratchets upward. More effort becomes too much effort. Over time, *passivity becomes not only tolerated, but normalised.*

This raises uncomfortable but necessary questions about the long-term implications of technological dependence. What happens to a generation that never learns to memorise directions, hold information in working memory, or compose thoughts without auto-suggestion? What does it mean to grow up in a world where initiative is rarely required and rarely rewarded? These are not theoretical concerns. They are practical, developmental, and urgent. The habits formed through repeated assistance will shape the cognitive landscape of the future—and, by extension, the societies that emerge from it.

Yet recognising this dynamic is not a call for wholesale rejection of technology. The aim is discernment, not disavowal. *Help must be examined, not eliminated.* What matters is whether we remain aware of when we are being helped, why, and at what cost. Systems that disclose their mechanisms, that prompt reflection, that invite interaction rather than override it—these are the kinds of tools that preserve agency while enhancing capacity. They support thinking rather than replacing it.

At the individual level, this means cultivating awareness around patterns of passive dependence. When reaching for a device to answer a question, pause: could you retrieve the information yourself? When relying on predictive text, ask: are you accepting the suggestion because it's accurate, or because it's easy? When following a recommended path, consider: is this your choice, or the system's assumption? These micro-moments are where autonomy is either reinforced or eroded. *The habit of help is not dangerous because it exists. It is dangerous because it disappears from view.*

To remain cognitively active in a world of automated assistance is not to reject help, but to use it consciously. It is to remember that skills, once unused, fade; that knowledge, once unpractised, becomes inaccessible; and that agency, once surrendered, rarely returns without effort. In the end, we do not merely become what we think. We become how we think—actively, or not at all.

The Myth of More Time

Time, we are told, is the great gift of technology. Every innovation—whether it's a voice assistant, an AI scheduler, or a next-generation microwave—comes wrapped in the promise of time saved. A few clicks replace a phone call. A swipe eliminates the need for conversation. Entire workflows are compressed into scripts and automations. In this vision, modern technology appears as a benevolent force, unburdening us of life's minor inefficiencies and returning hours back to our day. But look closer, and the promised surplus of time begins to dissolve under scrutiny. *We are saving time, certainly—but only in the abstract. What we are losing, in practice, is depth.*

The idea that technology liberates us by saving time rests on a measurable but misleading premise: that faster completion of tasks automatically equates to more time for what matters. In reality, what often follows is not freedom, but fragmentation. The time we 'gain' is rarely reallocated toward meaningful focus, creative thought, or even rest. Instead, it is more often redistributed across a greater number of micro-demands—notifications, prompts, recommendations, low-value tasks. The cognitive space we hoped to reclaim is repackaged and resold to us as opportunity: more to consume, more to monitor, more to respond to. *Our hours may be less encumbered by chores, but they are more crowded with interruptions.*

Consider the smartphone, arguably the most celebrated time-saving device of our age. It consolidates dozens of functions—communication, navigation, information retrieval, entertainment—into a single tool. Tasks that once took effort and scheduling are now instantaneous. Yet few users would describe themselves as having more free time than before. Quite the opposite: we are constantly 'checking', habitually grazing on updates, toggling between tabs of attention. Psychologists call this *continuous partial attention*—a state in which one is never fully present in any one activity because attention is constantly being recruited elsewhere. The net result is not spaciousness, but perpetual mental compression.

This is the fundamental bait-and-switch of the digital promise: that *efficiency leads to freedom*. In practice, what often results is a different kind of captivity—one not of hours spent, but of attention diluted. As Herbert Simon, the

Nobel Prize-winning economist, wrote as early as 1971, "a wealth of information creates a poverty of attention." What Simon could not have foreseen is the scale at which digital systems would compete for our attention, or the extent to which their design would monetise its fragmentation. Each interaction is engineered not only to be fast, but to leave a residue of engagement—a click, a swipe, a reaction, a cue. These fragments accumulate, not in duration but in cognitive load. *We are not saving time; we are scattering it.*

Behavioural research supports this dynamic. A study from the University of California, Irvine, found that knowledge workers typically switch tasks every three minutes and take an average of 23 minutes to return to the original task after an interruption. Notably, these interruptions are often self-initiated—driven by the very tools designed to make work more efficient. Email notifications, messaging platforms, shared calendars: each provides marginal gains in speed but collectively fractures the continuity of thought. What emerges is not just a distracted worker, but a mind trained to avoid sustained effort. *Speed becomes the default; depth becomes the anomaly.*

This isn't merely an issue of workflow. It represents a fundamental shift in how we experience time itself. In traditional cultures, time was often understood cyclically—tied to rituals, seasons, and rhythms of communal life. In modern industrial society, it became linear and commodified—divided into quantifiable units of productivity. In digital culture, time is increasingly experienced as *accelerated and compressed,* but also *dissolved.* We don't feel ourselves moving through time as much as we feel time collapsing into a constant now: alerts, updates, feeds without end. Philosopher Hartmut Rosa calls this "social acceleration"—the sense that everything is happening faster, yet we are falling further behind. *It is not that we have less time; it is that we have lost our grip on what time is for.*

This helps explain the paradox at the heart of modern productivity: that despite the proliferation of time-saving tools, many people feel more rushed, more overloaded, and more distracted than ever before. Part of the explanation lies in how technology redefines the scope of what's possible in a given unit of time. When tasks that once took thirty minutes now take five, the expectation is not that we enjoy the surplus—it is that we fill it with six other tasks. In other words, *efficiency increases expectations,* not peace. The measure of success becomes throughput, not satisfaction. Time is 'saved' only to be reinvested in doing more.

This dynamic is visible even in the language of work. Terms like *optimisation, scaling,* and *productivity hacks* dominate the discourse. Rarely is time discussed in terms of *meaning, attention,* or *presence.* Yet these are precisely the qualities that make time feel expansive. Psychologists refer to this as the difference between *clock time* and *lived time.* Clock time is measured externally—in minutes, schedules, and deadlines. Lived time is internal, subjective—how we experience the passage of time. A single hour of focused conversation can feel more substantial than an entire day spent switching between tasks. But convenience culture conditions us to favour clock time. We conflate speed with efficiency, forgetting that *not everything worth doing can—or should—be done faster.*

Even leisure has not escaped this logic. Streaming services automatically queue the next episode before credits have rolled. Algorithmic feeds offer content without prompting. Social platforms are engineered for frictionless scrolling. What passes for rest is often just another form of *passive stimulation*—not recovery, but occupation. The result is a leisure experience that mimics the tempo of work: continuous, shallow, consumptive. We don't feel restored by it, because it rarely allows for the mental deceleration that true rest requires. *Rest, like thought, takes time to become real.*

There is also a developmental cost to time fragmentation, particularly in young people. Emerging research suggests that growing up in an environment of constant digital stimulation affects not only attention span, but also emotional regulation and narrative memory. When time is experienced primarily in fragments, it becomes harder to build coherent stories—about the self, about the world, about cause and consequence. Education, which relies on sustained attention and delayed gratification, becomes more difficult. So does creativity, which depends on boredom, incubation, and the long simmer of unconscious processing. *The myth of more time is not only failing to deliver—*

it's actively narrowing the cognitive capacities it promised to expand.

It is worth asking: what would it mean to genuinely gain time, rather than merely accelerate it? It would not mean doing more, faster. It would mean reclaiming the ability to attend, to choose, to dwell. It would mean designing systems that preserve the texture of thought rather than slicing it into thinner and thinner slivers. It would require resisting the cultural impulse to measure every activity in terms of time saved, and instead ask what the saved time is *for*.

Such a reorientation would not entail rejecting technology, but using it with architectural intent. Tools should serve as temporal scaffolding—not as accelerants, but as structures that *protect and prioritise attention*. This might mean building in digital 'pauses' rather than eliminating them. It might mean accepting friction as a design principle, not an error. Most of all, it would mean *valuing time not only as a resource, but as a medium of thought*.

The reality is that time cannot truly be saved. It can only be spent differently. And in a culture obsessed with acceleration, the most radical act may be to stop, to linger, to resist the urgency of the next. Because it is not just how much time we have that matters. It is what our minds are doing while it passes. And on that front, the age of convenience has not delivered more time—it has only carved it into pieces small enough to be squandered.

Chapter 2
GPS for the Mind

Every street we no longer memorise, every direction we no longer plot ourselves, carries a subtle cognitive toll—one that is rarely apparent in the moment, yet accrues steadily over time. In a world where digital navigation has become second nature, we are quietly losing the capacity to orient ourselves independently. The convenience of perpetual locational certainty has displaced an older, embodied form of knowing: the art of being somewhere, consciously and attentively.

Not so long ago, navigating a city—or even a neighbourhood—was an active dialogue with one's surroundings. Streets were committed to memory; landmarks indexed mentally; detours became puzzles to solve, rather than glitches to be recalculated. Every journey layered sensory, cognitive, and emotional cues: the uneven pavement beneath a shortcut, the faded mural signalling the next turn, the aroma of a bakery confirming proximity. Wayfinding was not incidental; it was an exercise of attention, memory, and decision-making. Today, for countless people, that mental labour has been outsourced entirely.

The smartphone's capacity to dissolve spatial uncertainty is lauded as a major achievement, and in practical terms, it is. Real-time guidance reduces anxiety, extends mobility, and eases access to unfamiliar terrain. Yet beneath the surface of convenience lies a profound transformation. The moment-by-moment cognitive work that once structured human navigation has been replaced by a passive, screen-mediated experience. Neuroscience increasingly indicates that this shift is far from neutral: it alters the hippocampus, the brain region central to spatial memory, contextual awareness, and narrative construction.

Research at University College London revealed that habitual use of GPS navigation diminishes hippocampal engagement during wayfinding. Unlike traditional navigation, which compels the brain to construct and update an internal map from landmarks, orientation, and decision-points, digital systems offer linear guidance that circumvents these neural processes. Over time, this can affect not only spatial reasoning but also episodic memory and long-term learning. By surrendering the act of mapping to a device, we risk eroding the very architecture that underpins memory itself.

The implications extend beyond neural activity; they affect our lived experience of place. Streets, squares, and parks are more than backdrops—they are repositories of cues, context, and memory. Yet when mediated through screens, space flattens. "Turn left in 200 metres. Follow the blue line." Landmarks lose meaning; side streets blur into anonymity. We no longer cultivate spatial understanding; we consume directions, point by point.

This abstraction produces cognitive disembodiment. Movement ceases to be accompanied by thought. Embodied cognition, which recognises the integral role of body and environment in mental processes, shows that learning and memory are reinforced by gesture, exploration, and spatial engagement. Children who gesture retain knowledge more effectively; adults who physically trace routes remember better than those who merely observe. Navigation is not a set of coordinates—it is lived experience. Remove the effort, and the body disengages, the mind follows, and the world becomes less comprehensible.

Wayfinding has historically been entwined with survival, storytelling, and identity. In oral traditions, navigation was narrative: landmarks carried stories; routes encoded memory. Indigenous Australian songlines, for instance, map the land through song, embedding each verse in environmental features. Algorithmic navigation, in contrast, strips away narrative. We reach our destinations, but the journey leaves little trace in memory. Each step is efficient, but ephemeral.

This erosion extends into temporal continuity and personal history. Self-directed navigation creates stories: the unexpected detour, the discovery of a shortcut, the lesson in misjudgement. Such narratives anchor us in time and space, offering reflection, adaptation, and insight. Digital guidance, by design, eliminates deviation, replacing contingency with certainty. The result is a compressed, predictable experience—a subtle erasure of narrative richness.

The issue is not digital navigation itself, but the shift from active engagement to passive following—from agent to algorithmic subject. Over time, reliance on memory wanes, problem-solving diminishes, and exposure to micro-challenges that strengthen adaptive thinking is reduced. When we disengage mentally, emotionally, and sensorily from space, we forfeit one of the richest cognitive terrains available.

There are, of course, exceptions. For individuals with spatial impairments or high navigational anxiety, GPS offers genuine empowerment. In emergencies or time-critical coordination, it is indispensable. The distinction is intent: used thoughtfully, navigation technology is prosthetic; used uncritically, it becomes replacement. The boundary is narrow but meaningful.

What is lost is more than orientation—it is confidence: spatial, cognitive, existential. To navigate without a device is to exercise quiet authority, to affirm one's ability to engage with complexity. It situates the self within the environment, not as a passive observer but as an active reader of place. Knowledge of this sort cannot be downloaded or delegated; it must be earned through attention, observation, and movement.

This chapter begins with a simple premise: the decline of wayfinding is a symptom of a broader cognitive shift. We trade spatial intelligence for convenience, and in doing so, forfeit more than we immediately recognise. The ability to navigate independently cultivates memory, decision-making, and agency—it binds selfhood to the external architecture of the world.

What follows is an exploration of this tradeoff—neurologically, behaviourally, and culturally. The aim is not to reject GPS outright, but to reclaim effort as a cognitive act. Navigating actively, rather than passively, is more than reaching a destination; it is the reinforcement of memory, agency, and the mind-body-world connection. In a society increasingly structured around passivity, choosing to find your own way remains one of the most radical acts of thinking available.

Losing Our Mental Maps

In the age of digital certainty, we rarely ask for directions. The blue dot on our screens tells us where we are, and a glowing line tells us where to go. We follow instructions not with curiosity but with compliance, rarely glancing up to orient ourselves by landmarks, rarely engaging in the mental work of navigation. For millions of people, finding one's way has ceased to be a cognitive task; it is now a service outsourced to algorithms. But this shift carries a cost. *The less we navigate, the less we retain our capacity to know where we are—mentally, spatially, and contextually.*

For most of human history, wayfinding was a primary cognitive task. It demanded attention, pattern recognition, memory, and problem-solving. Navigating unfamiliar terrain required constructing mental maps, noticing irregularities, inferring connections, and remembering sequences. Our brains evolved to meet these demands. Anthropological research reveals that even pre-literate cultures developed extraordinary spatial acuity, relying on sun position, environmental cues, and geographic features to travel long distances without tools. What we now consider a challenge—finding a street in a new city—was once a basic human competence, and one tied intimately to a specific region of the brain: the hippocampus.

The hippocampus is not simply a memory centre; it is a spatial engine. Functional imaging studies have shown that this structure plays a crucial role in building what neuroscientists call "cognitive maps"—internal representations of physical space that allow for navigation, orientation, and spatial memory. In 2014, research conducted at University College London revealed that London taxi drivers, who must memorise thousands of routes and landmarks to pass "The Knowledge," exhibit increased grey matter volume in the posterior hippocampus. This structural change is not innate—it emerges through training and use. Conversely, studies have found that reduced engagement in spatial tasks correlates with decreased hippocampal activity, and over time, atrophy. *When navigation is offloaded to a device, the very system responsible for spatial thought begins to degrade through disuse.*

Digital navigation, by its nature, eliminates the need to form a mental map. Rather than constructing an internal representation of the route, users follow step-by-step prompts. This is procedural memory, not spatial memory. The distinction is critical. Procedural memory allows us to follow a recipe or perform a routine. Spatial memory allows us to infer, adapt, and improvise. A person who knows the shape of a city can reorient after a detour. A person who has only followed instructions cannot. The implications go beyond mere convenience—they speak to how we experience the world. *Navigation is not just about reaching a destination; it is about knowing how things relate to one another in space—and, by extension, how we relate to our environment.*

There is also a behavioural shift tied to this offloading. As people rely more heavily on GPS, they begin to pay less attention to their surroundings. Researchers at McGill University found that individuals navigating with turn-by-turn instructions were significantly less likely to recall landmarks, notice changes in environment, or retain information about the route. This diminished situational awareness is not an incidental side effect—it is a structural consequence of attentional redirection. When the mind trusts that it will be told what to do next, it stops attending to what is around it. This creates a peculiar kind of presence: the body is in space, but the mind is elsewhere—awaiting its next instruction.

This form of cognitive detachment is compounded by design. Navigation apps encourage a kind of tunnel vision, visually and cognitively. Users fixate on the screen, tracking their icon's progress along a predefined path. Real-world information becomes subordinate to the digital overlay. A person walking through a city might pass churches, parks, murals, and markets without registering any of them. The richness of place is replaced by a minimal interface: arrival time, distance remaining, next turn. *Space becomes data—something to be processed, not experienced.*

The long-term effects of this shift are still being studied, but early indicators are concerning. In 2020, a team of cognitive neuroscientists published findings showing that older adults who relied on GPS navigation had significantly poorer spatial recall than those who used maps or self-guided strategies. While causality remains complex, the association is strong enough to warrant attention. Spatial disorientation is an early sign of cognitive decline, particularly in diseases like Alzheimer's, which often target the hippocampus. Preserving spatial navigation skills may therefore be more than a matter of mental fitness—it may be protective against neurodegeneration. And yet we are systematically engineering those skills out of daily life.

This loss is not simply neurological—it is existential. Our sense of location is bound up with our sense of self. To know where you are is to be anchored in the world. To get lost, and then to find your way, is a powerful reaffirmation of agency. The experience of recovering orientation—of recognising a landmark, retracing steps, or triangulating a position—is cognitively and emotionally significant. It reminds us that we are capable of navigating complexity, of building internal coherence from external cues. It teaches adaptability, persistence, and inference. These are not trivial skills. They are the substrate of intelligence.

Moreover, the act of mapping—whether mental or physical—has always been a way of imposing meaning on space. A child who draws their route to school is not simply making a record; they are telling a story. They are identifying what matters. They are constructing a narrative of movement and memory. When that process is replaced by automated routing, the user becomes a passive traveller rather than an active wayfinder. Over time, *this erodes the habit of self-orientation*—not only geographically, but psychologically. It trains us to seek direction externally before attempting to locate ourselves internally.

This reorientation has cultural consequences as well. Across societies, spatial practices shape identity. Indigenous mapping traditions, for instance, integrate geography with mythology, ancestry, and social order. Even in modern urban life, neighbourhoods are not just physical zones—they are experiential territories, shaped by paths taken, places known, and routes remembered. When we no longer participate in constructing these mental geographies, we become less attached to place. A route driven daily with GPS feels less like a part of one's world than a corridor between locations. *The mind, unanchored, begins to treat space as a void to be crossed rather than a field to be understood.*

There are those who argue that offloading navigation frees cognitive resources for other, higher-order tasks. Why memorise routes when that energy can be applied to creative or analytical thinking? It's a compelling idea—but it rests on a false dichotomy. *Spatial cognition is not a primitive function to be discarded; it is foundational.* It supports working memory, visualisation, and strategic planning. Elite athletes, surgeons, architects, and musicians all rely on spatial skills. To cultivate them is not to regress—it is to reinforce a core dimension of intelligence.

The danger is not the tool, but the default. Navigation aids are immensely valuable when used intentionally—for exploration, efficiency, or reassurance. The problem arises when they become habitual replacements for thinking. As with any form of cognitive outsourcing, the question is not whether the tool works. It is whether it reshapes the user.

And in the case of navigation, the reshaping is literal: patterns of brain activity shift; attention narrows; spatial reasoning weakens.

To understand where you are is to understand *how* you are. It is a synthesis of memory, attention, and embodiment. And it is under quiet threat—not by design, but by omission. By the slow, steady erosion of spatial engagement through seamless automation. If we do not notice this loss, we will not resist it. If we do not resist it, we will forget that we ever knew our way. And when that happens, *our maps will not be the only thing missing—our sense of place in the world will go with them.*

The Vanishing of Landmarks

Landmarks used to matter. They weren't just incidental features of the environment—they were *anchors* of orientation, memory, and meaning. The red post box at the corner, the leaning tree near the school gate, the graffiti-covered wall that signalled the turn home—these weren't mere backdrops to movement; they were signposts of experience. In the analogue world, landmarks were cognitive waypoints, stitched together by memory to create a sense of space. They gave structure to our internal maps and helped us ground ourselves in unfamiliar terrain. Today, their role is diminishing. As navigation becomes increasingly screen-mediated, *the physical world loses its texture*. We see where we are going, but not what we're going through.

The rise of GPS-based navigation has not just changed how we find our way—it has changed what we notice. Instead of scanning the environment for cues, we fixate on a screen. The blue dot becomes our locus of attention, and the path it traces becomes the only relevant route. The world itself—its smells, shapes, asymmetries—fades into peripheral vision. We learn to follow, not to interpret. This is not a technological glitch; it is the intended design of convenience. Turn-by-turn instructions eliminate the need for personal wayfinding, and with it, *the motivation to attend to the environment* in any meaningful way.

Attention is the beginning of memory. When we stop noticing landmarks, we stop forming memories anchored to place. A study by Ishikawa et al. (2008) compared participants navigating a city using a GPS, a paper map, or no aid at all. Those using GPS formed the fewest mental representations of their environment and performed worst on spatial recall tests. The researchers concluded that GPS reduces users' reliance on environmental features and weakens spatial learning. In short, when the environment becomes passive, so do we. Landmarks don't just vanish from view; they vanish from memory.

This has implications beyond individual navigation. Our ability to recall where things are, how to get somewhere, or even what surrounds us is deeply tied to *situational awareness*. In urban settings, where environments are complex and dynamic, knowing one's bearings isn't just practical—it's protective. Landmarks offer redundancy when systems fail, orientation when signage is unclear, and context when direction becomes ambiguous. In emergency situations, people who have trained themselves to notice and encode environmental features are more likely to act decisively. The decline of landmark awareness isn't just a minor cultural shift; it erodes a key layer of cognitive resilience.

The relationship between landmarks and memory is also fundamental to how we construct narrative. Unlike digital directions, which are typically linear and minimal, spatial memories are associative and rich. Ask someone how they get to their favourite café and they'll often describe the journey in terms of landmarks—"past the old cinema," "just after the roundabout with the sculpture," "beside the shop that sells those amazing tarts." These descriptions aren't precise in a Cartesian sense, but they are *cognitively dense*. They embed movement within a web of references, values, and past experiences. Landmarks give life to routes. Without them, space becomes sterile—depersonalised and interchangeable.

This sterility is particularly evident in newer urban developments, where design prioritises functionality and symmetry over uniqueness and irregularity. Streets lined with identical façades and indistinguishable signage make orientation more difficult, not less. Kevin Lynch, in his seminal 1960 work *The Image of the City*, argued that a city's legibility—its ease of navigation and memorability—depends on the distinctiveness of its landmarks. A visually rich environment helps individuals create a mental map of their surroundings. When every building looks the same, or when visual complexity is flattened by digital mediation, we lose the features that help us attach memory to place.

Screen-based navigation contributes to this flattening in a subtler way. The standard navigation interface offers an abstracted version of the environment: clean lines, consistent icons, minimal clutter. It is designed for efficiency, not discovery. It tells us what to look for (the next turn, the estimated arrival time) and implicitly instructs us to ignore everything else. There is no space in this interface for the idiosyncratic or the unexpected. A mural, a crooked alley, a forgotten monument—none of these have relevance unless they serve a navigational function. But *irrelevance is often the birthplace of memory.* The features we remember most are not always those that were useful, but those that were distinctive, surprising, or emotionally resonant.

The emotional aspect of landmarks is often overlooked. Places acquire significance not just through function, but through repeated emotional association. The bench where you had an important conversation, the hill you climbed during a difficult time, the café you visited alone after moving to a new city—these are not coordinates, but *anchors of personal history.* They help us mark the passage of time and locate our experiences in the world. When we delegate navigation to devices, we risk short-circuiting the very process by which these emotional associations are formed.

Movement becomes efficient but forgettable. We get there, but nothing lingers.

There is also a social dimension to landmark awareness. Shared landmarks are the scaffolding of collective memory. Cities, in particular, derive much of their character from the accumulation of commonly recognised places. "Meet me by the lion statue," "He lives near the church with the clock tower," "It's just down from the old library"—these are not just directions; they are acts of communal orientation. They presume a shared knowledge of the built environment and a shared investment in its features. When navigation becomes purely individualised—mediated by personal devices and private interfaces—*the shared spatial vocabulary begins to erode*. We become co-inhabitants of the same space, but not co-navigators of a common place.

To be clear, the issue is not with the use of GPS or digital maps in themselves. These tools have opened access, improved efficiency, and enabled exploration. But their unchecked dominance has reshaped how we interact with the physical world. The real risk is not technological—it is cognitive. We are learning not to look. We are building habits of inattention. And when we stop attending, *we stop encoding*.

The vanishing of landmarks is not a passive loss—it is an active unlearning of spatial attentiveness. It reflects a broader cultural pattern in which external aids replace internal processes, and efficiency displaces engagement. But landmarks are not just waypoints—they are invitations.

They ask us to notice, to remember, and to connect. Their presence, or absence, tells us something profound about how we are living. If the world is starting to feel flatter, more generic, less vivid, it may not be because the world has changed. It may be because *we are no longer looking closely enough to see what anchors it.*

Embodied Thinking and Wayfinding

The act of finding one's way through the world has never been merely about geography. It is a form of thinking—an integration of perception, movement, memory, and judgement. And it is deeply *embodied.* To navigate without digital aid is to engage the full spectrum of cognitive faculties in dialogue with the body: reading subtle environmental cues, adjusting course in real time, building a mental model of surroundings by moving through space. Yet this kind of thinking is fast becoming unfamiliar. As digital navigation systems take over the heavy lifting of orientation, wayfinding is being reduced to passive following. What is lost is not just self-direction but a powerful mode of *embodied cognition*—a way of knowing that is enacted through movement and perception rather than abstract reasoning alone.

Embodied cognition is not a metaphor. It is a foundational concept in contemporary cognitive science that challenges the traditional notion of the brain as the sole seat of the mind. According to this view, cognition is not confined to the head but is distributed across the brain, body, and environment. Thought is shaped by bodily experience, sensory feedback, and physical interaction with the world. This framework has gained traction over the past three decades, supported by research across neuroscience, psychology, and philosophy. What we call "thinking" is not a detached, cerebral process—it is grounded in action, context, and sensorimotor experience.

Wayfinding offers one of the clearest and most consequential expressions of embodied cognition. When navigating without automated assistance, the individual is engaged in an ongoing loop of perception, decision-making, and motion. One scans the environment, recognises landmarks, estimates distances, adjusts for obstacles, updates orientation, and stores sequences for future recall. These processes are not linear—they are recursive and situated. They rely on multiple brain systems working in concert: the hippocampus (for spatial mapping), the parietal lobe (for sensory integration), the prefrontal cortex (for planning and decision-making), and the vestibular system (for balance and movement awareness). In active navigation, the brain does not simply think about the world—it *thinks with the world.*

This is why movement through space is cognitively enriching. Numerous studies have shown that physically navigating an environment strengthens memory, increases attention to detail, and enhances problem-solving skills. In one widely cited experiment, participants who physically explored a virtual environment performed significantly better on memory tests than those who viewed the same environment passively. Active engagement—not just visual exposure—was the key variable. The implications are profound. *We learn more when we move.* We remember more when we exert effort. And we understand more deeply when our thinking is grounded in physical action.

Digital navigation disrupts this loop. By externalising the decision-making process, it interrupts the embodied feedback mechanisms that foster cognitive development. The user is no longer required to construct a spatial model or remember previous cues. Instead, they are guided turn by turn, with the environment reduced to a secondary backdrop. This shift may seem trivial in a single instance, but its cumulative effects are anything but. Over time, consistent reliance on GPS systems weakens spatial memory, diminishes environmental awareness, and blunts decision-making skills. The brain learns that it need not engage fully, and so it doesn't.

This cognitive disengagement is not just theoretical. Neuroimaging studies have shown reduced activation in the hippocampus during GPS-guided navigation compared to self-guided wayfinding. In effect, the very region of the brain responsible for constructing spatial maps goes quiet when we hand over control to an algorithm. Given the hippocampus's role in both memory and navigation, this should raise concern. Shrinkage in this region has been linked not only to impaired spatial skills but also to early signs of neurodegenerative conditions such as Alzheimer's.

It is possible, then, that the erosion of embodied navigation is not only a cultural loss but a neurological risk.

But the consequences of disengaging from wayfinding are not only about brain health. They extend to *decision-making more broadly*. Navigation is fundamentally a series of decisions: when to turn, whether to adjust course, how to weigh alternatives under uncertainty. These are the micro-acts of judgement that cultivate executive function—our ability to plan, regulate, and adapt behaviour in complex contexts. When these decisions are offloaded to machines, we lose not only the opportunity to practise them but also the confidence that comes from having done so successfully. Over time, the habit of making decisions becomes unfamiliar, even aversive. And when decisions do arise—outside the domain of navigation—we may find ourselves less prepared to face them.

This is not an argument against digital assistance per se. There are valid and important reasons to use navigation tools—accessibility, safety, efficiency, or exposure to new routes. The issue is not the tool but the default. When every act of movement is accompanied by real-time guidance, the opportunity for embodied thinking is systematically removed. What begins as help becomes habit, and what becomes habit reshapes ability. The question is not whether GPS helps us reach our destination. It is whether it helps us *understand the journey*—spatially, cognitively, and experientially.

Embodied wayfinding does more than sharpen cognitive function. It anchors us in the world. It situates the self within a dynamic environment and fosters a sense of continuity between mind, body, and place. This sense of being *in* the world—not merely moving through it—is essential for psychological grounding. It creates a kind of cognitive humility: the awareness that the world does not yield itself instantly but must be explored, interpreted, and remembered. In a culture obsessed with immediacy and efficiency, such humility is countercultural. But it is precisely what fosters resilience and autonomy.

There are practical implications for how we might reclaim embodied wayfinding in daily life. Choosing to navigate a familiar route without GPS. Drawing maps from memory. Teaching children to orient themselves through physical cues rather than digital instructions. These are not nostalgic gestures. They are acts of cognitive investment. They reassert the link between movement and memory, between attention and understanding. And they restore the dignity of effort in a domain that has been flattened by automation.

One might object that these skills are simply outdated—that in a world of real-time data, self-guided navigation is inefficient. But this reflects a narrow view of efficiency, one that prioritises speed over synthesis. From an evolutionary perspective, humans did not develop their cognitive capacities by doing things quickly. They developed them by doing things *fully*—by engaging with uncertainty, building internal models, and adapting in response. Navigation was never a distraction from cognition; it was a training ground for it. The mental maps we build are not merely tools for travel—they are *frameworks for thinking*.

What is at stake, then, is more than spatial competence. It is the preservation of a mode of cognition that integrates perception, movement, and decision into a coherent whole. Embodied thinking is not a relic of a pre-digital past. It is a vital form of intelligence that deserves to be protected, cultivated, and revalued. In the context of wayfinding, it means resisting the flattening of experience into coordinates and commands. It means remembering that every path traced on foot is also a path traced in mind. And it means recognising that the shortest route is not always the richest one. *Sometimes, the act of finding our way is the very thing that shows us who we are.*

Beyond Directions: A Loss of Narrative

Knowing where you are has never been a matter of coordinates alone. It is a story, a structure, a sense of place built from memory, association, and movement. When we navigate through the world without assistance, we are not just plotting points on a map—we are *weaving a narrative* that links moments, decisions, and meanings into a coherent sense of lived experience. But as digital navigation tools automate that process, replacing embodied orientation with real-time instruction, we risk more than a loss of wayfinding ability. *We risk a collapse in the narrative architecture of spatial experience itself.*

At the heart of this loss is a displacement of continuity. Traditional navigation, whether by intuition, maps, or learned paths, requires the brain to track where it has been, anticipate where it is going, and maintain a thread of coherence throughout the journey. This thread is not trivial. It links space to memory and memory to identity. When you navigate actively, your route becomes part of your story. You remember that you turned left at the café with the green awning because it reminded you of a trip abroad. You recall that you got lost near the museum and stumbled upon a hidden bookshop. These are not waypoints; they are *chapters*. They place your body in time and space and anchor your experience in a geography that feels not only physical but personal.

The cognitive science behind this is unambiguous. The hippocampus, a structure central to spatial memory, is also instrumental in what neuroscientists call *episodic memory*—the ability to recall past experiences as sequences of events. It allows us to situate ourselves in time, construct autobiographical memory, and imagine future scenarios. Damage to the hippocampus impairs both navigation and narrative recall. This is not coincidental. It suggests that *spatial continuity and narrative continuity are intimately linked.* The ability to construct a coherent spatial model is entangled with the ability to construct a coherent sense of self.

When we outsource navigation to digital systems, we sever the need to generate that continuity. The turn-by-turn interface replaces holistic understanding with disjointed commands. The journey is reduced to a series of isolated prompts: turn left here, continue straight, arrive. The individual no longer builds a mental map but follows instructions reactively, without retaining a sense of trajectory or sequence. As a result, there is no path to remember, no story to tell. The geography we inhabit becomes invisible, reduced to what the screen deems relevant. *We arrive, but we do not recall the journey.*

This fragmentation extends beyond spatial orientation. It shapes how we process experience. Consider the contrast between walking through a neighbourhood you've navigated before and one guided by GPS. In the former, your attention is distributed—between landmarks, memories, visual cues, and ambient sounds. In the latter, your gaze is often fixed on a glowing screen, waiting for the next command. The environment is encountered in fragments, prompted by the interface, and discarded once the instruction is fulfilled. Psychologically, this interrupts the construction of narrative. There is no unfolding arc, no accumulation of impressions, only a series of micro-decisions made on your behalf.

The broader consequence is a thinning of spatial narrative—our internalised sense of how places connect, how movement feels, and how memory attaches to geography. As spatial psychologist Colin Ellard argues, environments matter not only because of what they contain but because of how they *structure experience over time*. Streets, buildings, and open spaces act as prompts for memory and meaning. When movement through those spaces is automated, we stop encoding the associations that make them memorable. We lose what he calls "environmental narrative": the rich interplay between setting, action, and identity that transforms wayfinding into story-making.

This erosion is particularly consequential in urban contexts, where our sense of self is often scaffolded by spatial familiarity. City dwellers identify not just with their homes, but with their commutes, their local haunts, their habitual routes. These spaces are part of their cognitive identity. They encode routines, mark transitions, and offer continuity in otherwise dynamic environments. When GPS intervenes, especially in daily life, it can flatten this spatial texture. Instead of building a mental map layered with emotion and memory, the user becomes a transient dot moving across a sterile grid. *They are present, but not placed.*

Moreover, the absence of spatial narrative impairs not only memory but also imagination. Psychologist Eleanor Maguire, known for her work on London taxi drivers, has shown that the hippocampus is active not just when remembering past routes but when *simulating future ones*. This ability to mentally project ourselves forward—known as "prospective memory"—is essential to planning, problem-solving, and storytelling. It allows us to ask, "What happens next?" and build narratives from anticipated outcomes. But without a grasp of spatial continuity, this simulation becomes more difficult. The individual may know where they're going but lack the mental scaffolding to imagine how they'll get there or what it will mean.

The impact is generational. For children and young adults raised on GPS, spatial narrative is not simply underused—it is underdeveloped. Fewer opportunities exist to get lost, to improvise, to make decisions that are remembered because they were consequential. Instead, navigation is often pre-scripted, with parents tracking locations and digital tools preventing deviation. The result is not just safer travel but more linear, less storied experience. The unexpected, the misremembered, the coincidental—these narrative ingredients are filtered out by systems designed for efficiency. *In removing friction, we also remove texture.*

Some might argue that digital tools simply replace one kind of narrative with another—that the screen-mediated experience offers its own stories, layered with data, history, and metadata. And to a limited extent, this is true. Augmented reality apps can enrich place-based experience; map overlays can visualise temporal change. But these narratives are curated from outside. They are not generated by the user through interaction, movement, and interpretation. What is lost is *authorship*. The individual ceases to be the narrator of their own spatial experience and becomes a consumer of pre-structured data. Even when stories are present, they are not *lived*.

This has implications for collective memory as well. Public history is often tied to shared spaces and the stories embedded within them. Monuments, streets, squares, and thoroughfares are not just infrastructure—they are narrative containers. They tell of migrations, resistances, economies, and identities. When navigation bypasses these spaces, or renders them invisible to the user, it contributes to a subtle but meaningful erosion of collective awareness. The historical, the political, the cultural—these dimensions of place require attention. And attention requires presence, not just passage.

To navigate actively is to engage in a form of personal authorship. It is to decide, to observe, to remember, and to infer. These acts are not just cognitive—they are narrative. They bind events into sequences, sequences into memory, and memory into identity. Without them, we risk losing not only our sense of direction but our sense of *continuity*. We may know where we are in the moment, but we may forget where we've been, or why it mattered. And without that thread, *the self becomes harder to locate.*

This is the unspoken cost of hyper-convenient navigation. It delivers us efficiently but denies us the opportunity to compose meaning along the way. It replaces spatial unfolding with pre-ordained steps. And in doing so, it removes one of the oldest forms of storytelling humans have known: the story of movement through space. Reclaiming that story does not require rejecting technology. It requires choosing to *notice,* to *participate,* and to *remember.* Because when we stop navigating, we don't just lose the map—we lose the plot.

Chapter 3
Predictive Everything

Rewrite the following article to pass AI-detection tools while retaining its professional, intellectually engaging, and authoritative tone.

Rephrase and restructure the content to feel human-authored, with a writing style that reflects the subtle imperfections and expressive flow of a skilled writer.

Specifically: – Vary sentence structures, paragraph rhythms, and transition choices to avoid algorithmic patterns

– Introduce occasional conversational touches or rhetorical asides where appropriate

– Make subtle word choices or phrase shifts that sound natural but aren't statistically predictable

– Avoid "perfectly smooth" sentence-to-sentence transitions—a little friction is more human

– Maintain the original meaning, flow, facts, and paragraphing

– Do not simplify or summarise—this is not a paraphrasing task, but a creative re-authorship

– Use British English conventions

– Ensure the result still reads like it was written by a seasoned nonfiction writer with intellectual and emotional depth

Output only the reworked article text. No explanations. No headers. No setup language.

There is a particular seduction in being anticipated. To have one's thoughts pre-empted, one's needs prefigured, one's desires guessed before they are fully formed. It offers the illusion of intimacy and the comfort of efficiency. Autocomplete finishes our sentences. Autofill completes our forms. Predictive playlists know what we want to hear. Recommendation engines predict what we'll want next—what to buy, where to eat, who to follow, even how we're likely to feel. And while these systems promise to make life smoother, faster, and more responsive, they also carry a subtle but profound cost: the erosion of original intention. In a world optimised to guess what comes next, the very process of thinking for oneself is being quietly deprioritised.

Predictive technology is not a passive convenience. It is a form of cognitive design. By reducing the effort needed to complete tasks, it reshapes the way we approach language, decisions, and meaning-making. Take, for example, the experience of writing an email or text. As predictive suggestions flash across the screen, they do more than help. They prompt. They influence. A sentence begins in your voice and ends in a template. Over time, that template becomes familiar, even habitual. You start deferring not just out of laziness, but because the suggestion seems close enough—"That'll do." Except it isn't quite you. And after hundreds, even thousands, of these interactions, the line between your thoughts and the system's best guesses begins to blur.

This is not merely a linguistic issue. It is a cognitive shift. When our tools intervene too early in the process of thought formation, they don't just accelerate our expression—they truncate it. They reward speed over depth, completion over reflection. Instead of wrestling with ambiguity, searching for the right word, or revisiting an idea to shape it more precisely, we accept the first prompt that appears plausible. The result is a kind of intellectual atrophy. As the tools become smarter, we become more docile—less likely to pause, consider, and reframe.

The behavioural psychologist B.F. Skinner once noted that the most powerful reinforcements are intermittent and anticipatory. Predictive systems operate in much the same way. They create a feedback loop in which suggestion and acceptance become entangled. Each time we accept an autocomplete phrase, we reinforce the system's model and train ourselves to outsource. We adapt to the interface as much as it adapts to us. And because these exchanges occur at such a granular level, they often evade scrutiny. It feels like we are just typing faster, responding quicker, getting things done. But what is being edited out of our thinking when we never have to finish a sentence on our own?

Consider the architecture of digital interfaces—the dropdown menus, the prepopulated fields, the search predictions. Each of these elements narrows a field of possibility into a set of options. They seem to offer choice, but in fact they are pre-curated constraints. This is the logic of "choice architecture," a term popularised by behavioural economists like Richard Thaler and Cass Sunstein. Every interface design presents options in a way that nudges behaviour—often imperceptibly. Where a form places the "default" option, how a search engine ranks results, or how an app auto-suggests replies are not neutral decisions. They shape what we notice, what we prioritise, and ultimately what we choose.

Yet these nudges occur beneath the threshold of conscious deliberation. The user experiences them as helpful guidance, not as cognitive limitation. The danger lies in what is not presented—paths not suggested, ideas not surfaced, alternatives never known. The interface becomes a filter for thought, replacing the mental openness of "What do I think?" with the reactive rhythm of "What's suggested?" The more we engage with predictive systems, the more our decisions are subtly nudged from within the framework those systems define.

This is not simply a design issue. It is a matter of cognitive ecology—the environment in which thought takes shape. When the ecology is dominated by reactive prompts, our thinking becomes shallow, fragmented, and less exploratory. The philosopher Jiddu Krishnamurti once observed that the ability to observe without evaluating is the highest form of intelligence. But predictive systems are designed to do the opposite: to evaluate constantly, to intervene pre-emptively, and to offer shortcuts that short-circuit observation altogether.

A striking example of this shift is evident in the way we search for information. Where once a question might prompt reflection, reading, and synthesis, it now often leads to a quick search and an algorithmically ranked list of answers. The top results are clicked, skimmed, and accepted. But rarely is the structure of the ranking questioned. Why was that answer at the top? What wasn't shown? What assumptions did the search autocomplete encode into the query itself? These are not just epistemological concerns—they are existential ones. Because when the search begins with a predictive suggestion, it often ends with a preordained conclusion. The journey of thought is pre-contracted.

In professional and academic contexts, this has consequences beyond personal convenience. When predictive systems intrude into research platforms, legal databases, or medical diagnostics, they shape not only what is found, but what is asked. A scientist searching for literature may be nudged toward dominant paradigms. A clinician using diagnostic support may miss rare conditions that don't fit predictive models. A policy analyst relying on AI-curated summaries may miss the nuance buried in less visible sources. In each case, prediction doesn't merely supplement cognition—it steers it.

And then there is the emotional domain. Predictive text and recommendation systems are increasingly present in our personal lives—in relationships, self-reflection, and communication. Messaging platforms now offer one-tap replies like "Thanks!" or "Sounds good." While these options save time, they also collapse affective nuance. A subtle difference in phrasing—"Appreciate it" vs. "Thanks" vs. "I really mean it"—is lost. The reply becomes a signal of efficiency, not emotion. Over time, as we rely on these auto-replies, we may find ourselves emotionally flattened, less expressive, more generic.

The underlying problem is not that these systems exist. It is that we often accept their presence uncritically, without recognising what they displace. The intention to write, to think, to choose is replaced by reaction. And while reaction is faster, it is rarely deeper. The process of forming an idea—testing it, rejecting it, finding better language, changing direction—is not a peripheral aspect of intelligence. It is intelligence. It is what makes thought alive, adaptive, and human.

When systems pre-empt our thinking, we lose this inner rehearsal. We move from thinking in time to thinking on rails. Our minds shift from exploring the terrain of possibility to riding the groove of prediction. And though we may still feel autonomous—after all, we can always ignore the suggestion—every interface carries with it an implied recommendation: that stopping to think is optional, and perhaps even inefficient.

But the cost of this efficiency is real. It is not just the loss of originality. It is the weakening of the very mechanisms that generate originality in the first place. Like muscles unexercised, the faculties of critical thought, imaginative leap, and conceptual revision atrophy when they are rarely used. What emerges in their place is not stupidity, but mental passivity. A soft, subtle erosion of cognitive ambition, disguised as convenience.

And so this chapter takes us into the predictive landscape—not to argue against the utility of these tools, but to examine what they assume, what they reward, and what they risk. It asks what kind of thinkers we become when our sentences are always half-written for us, when our choices are quietly managed by interface logic, and when the friction of forming a thought is treated not as a feature of intelligence, but as a flaw in user experience.

The challenge before us is not to discard predictive technology, but to reclaim intentionality. To resist the automatic when it matters. To dwell in the discomfort of uncertainty when meaning is at stake. To type the harder sentence. To choose the unprompted word. Because in those moments—unpredictable, effortful, unrehearsed—we do not merely complete our thoughts. We become authors of them.

The Lure of Autocomplete

Midway through a sentence—before the thought has fully formed—your device offers a suggestion. "Let me know if..." becomes "you need anything." You pause, glance, and tap. The reply is polite, efficient, and somehow not entirely yours. It works. You send it. But something has shifted. The friction of crafting expression has been replaced by the acceptance of convenience. This is the quiet power of predictive text: not to shape what we write, but *how we think about writing in the first place.*

Autocomplete is among the most ubiquitous cognitive interfaces in modern life. It completes our emails, messages, searches, and, increasingly, our thoughts. Initially marketed as a benign timesaver—streamlining mundane tasks like typing or form-filling—it has evolved into a behavioural scaffold. Behind its surface lies a powerful feedback system: one that learns from us, predicts us, and gradually teaches us to prefer efficiency over articulation. As it becomes normal to accept rather than compose, the boundaries between assistance and authorship blur. The subtle consequence is this: *we become editors of a script we didn't write.*

The persuasive pull of autocomplete is rooted in what psychologists call *cognitive economy*. Our brains are naturally inclined to conserve energy, especially when tasks are familiar or low-stakes. Predictive tools exploit this tendency, offering just-in-time completions that feel like minor victories—less typing, faster responses, fewer decisions. But what they save in labour, they often cost in engagement. A 2020 study published in *Nature Human Behaviour* found that predictive text not only influences the length and style of written communication but also subtly shifts its tone and content to conform with the system's learned norms. In essence, predictive systems mirror the statistical average of human language back to us—and we begin to imitate that average in return.

The phenomenon is not limited to keyboards. Consider search engines. A user begins typing a query: "Is it normal to..." and before finishing, the system proposes a dozen completions based on previous search behaviour and aggregate data. These suggestions don't merely speed up access—they *shape the question itself*. The initial curiosity may have been vague or nuanced, but the autocomplete funnel nudges it into a recognisable mould. What is statistically probable begins to define what is intellectually possible. The danger here is not misinformation, but *premature closure*: the truncation of a thought process before it can deepen or diversify.

This effect accumulates. Day by day, interaction by interaction, users become more habituated to accepting suggestions over initiating original inputs. It becomes reflexive. The internal voice of composition—once shaped by memory, imagination, and context—begins to outsource its first drafts to the machine. In doing so, a cognitive dependency forms: *a learned reliance on the system to scaffold not just our sentences, but our sequencing of thought*. Language becomes less exploratory and more templated, not because we are incapable of originality, but because the path of least resistance leads elsewhere.

The implications stretch beyond communication. Autocomplete trains us in *anticipatory compliance*. We begin to trust the system's next move, not because we've assessed its merit, but because it arrives faster than our own. The delay that once invited deliberation now feels inefficient. Thought becomes reactive. The moment we hesitate, the system fills the silence, and we, relieved to be relieved of the effort, surrender the moment of struggle—the friction where insight lives. This surrender is not malicious or foolish; it is ambient and ambiently encouraged.

The neuroscientific underpinnings of this shift are both sobering and instructive. The prefrontal cortex—the seat of executive function, reasoning, and working memory—is activated when we construct original thoughts or revise them through effort. It is less active when we rely on stored patterns or external prompts. When predictive systems intervene early in a task, they *bypass this activation*, offering fast resolution without cortical engagement. Over time, this can result in what researchers term "disuse weakening"—a measurable decrease in neural efficiency related to skills that are underexercised. The brain, ever adaptive, shifts resources elsewhere. The more we let the machine think for us, the less our own cognitive circuits are enlisted.

And yet, the issue is not whether predictive tools are inherently bad. They are not. In contexts of accessibility, multilingual communication, or time-sensitive scenarios, they offer genuine value. The problem arises when these tools are *frictionless by design and mindless by habit*. When the baseline expectation becomes "fast, familiar, and acceptable," rather than "thoughtful, precise, and new," we risk cultivating a culture of *cognitive inertia*. We don't just save time; we *unlearn initiative*.

This shift is evident in professional environments as well. Consider customer service agents who use canned responses suggested by AI, or journalists who rely on autocomplete features in content management systems, or educators drafting feedback guided by predictive language models. In each case, there is a trade-off between speed and specificity. The danger is not that work becomes less human, but that the *human elements become standardised*. Feedback starts to sound the same. Emails become indistinguishable. Language is stripped of idiosyncrasy—not by censorship, but by *statistical blandness*.

Critics might argue that this concern is overblown, that predictive systems merely accelerate tasks we've already decided to complete. But this assumes a clean separation between *intention* and *expression*—a separation that cognitive science no longer supports. Expression is *generative*. The act of writing shapes the idea being written. To predict a sentence before it has been formed is to subtly alter what is being formed at all. Language is not a conveyor belt—it is a forge. And predictive tools, by intervening too early, risk cooling the fire before the shape has emerged.

There are cultural ramifications too. Autocomplete doesn't simply accelerate communication; it flattens it. In a global, interconnected world where platforms prioritise uniformity and scale, predictive language systems tend toward *linguistic convergence*—the median tone, the safest idiom, the least risky phrasing. Over time, regionalisms fade, stylistic flourishes recede, and voice becomes formulaic. What we gain in mutual legibility, we may lose in expressive diversity. We begin to sound alike—not because we are alike, but because our tools have converged on the same models of prediction.

Yet perhaps the most insidious effect of autocomplete is not its influence on what we write, but on what we *don't*. The hesitation that once prompted reflection is now bypassed. The half-thought, once worthy of contemplation, is now buried under a tap-to-complete suggestion. The tentative phrasing, which once signalled uncertainty and vulnerability, is replaced with polished, overly certain prose. We become fluent in forms that preclude doubt. And this is no small loss. *Original thought does not emerge fully formed; it gropes, stumbles, iterates.* To accept a suggestion too early is to cut that process short.

To preserve the integrity of thought, we must reinstate friction as a feature, not a flaw. The delay before a word arrives is not wasted time—it is *thinking in action*. The silence before a response is not absence—it is presence. In resisting the automatic, we reclaim the formative terrain of cognition: the messiness, the revision, the risk of saying something new. And in doing so, we reassert the value of *voice*—not as performance, but as process.

Autocomplete, like any tool, is neutral only in theory. In practice, it reflects assumptions about what matters: speed over subtlety, ease over effort, completion over exploration. To use it wisely is to remain aware of those assumptions and to choose, at least some of the time, to type the sentence yourself—not because the suggestion is wrong, but because *what comes next should be yours to find*.

Choice Architecture and Its Biases

When you open a streaming platform and see a row of "Top Picks for You," followed by "Trending Now," "Continue Watching," and "Because You Watched," your gaze doesn't scan hundreds of titles—it follows a path someone else has laid out. The same occurs when you search for flights, browse news feeds, or select privacy settings. You're choosing—but not from a blank slate. Your options have already been arranged, weighted, and framed. *This is not accidental; it's architecture.* Specifically, *choice architecture*—the structured environment in which decisions are made. And like all architecture, it channels movement, shapes experience, and leaves certain directions harder to reach.

Coined by behavioural economists Richard Thaler and Cass Sunstein, the term "choice architecture" refers to the way in which choices are presented to us, and how that presentation can predictably influence our decisions. A classic example is organ donation policies: countries with an opt-out system tend to have far higher donor rates than those requiring opt-in, not because citizens differ in morality, but because *the default matters*. Defaults are sticky. Visibility matters. Order matters. And in digital environments, these factors are increasingly orchestrated not by public policy or design ethics, but by opaque algorithms optimised for engagement, revenue, or behavioural prediction.

The digital shift in choice architecture is not merely a change in form—it's a transformation of *function*. In physical environments, choice architecture is often static and visible: store layouts, traffic signs, menu designs. Online, it is dynamic, personalised, and invisible. Your version of a shopping site differs from mine—not just in branding or ads, but in *what choices appear, when, and how*. Predictive interfaces quietly curate our decision-making scaffolds, narrowing our exposure to complexity and subtly *biasing our perception of what's available or worth considering.*

The result is not just nudged behaviour—it's *a reframed sense of what exists.*

This phenomenon is particularly potent when digital systems suppress *negative friction*—the small resistances that prompt reflection or pause. A checkout screen with a single "Buy Now" button removes the friction of second-guessing. A dating app with a swipe-right default removes the pause of curiosity. A "Skip Intro" button preempts a conscious decision to watch or wait. These designs are not malicious; they're optimised for flow. But in doing so, they *collapse the space in which intention might arise*. They don't merely assist decisions—they *pre-empt* them.

This leads to a deeper, less examined consequence: the suppression of independent reasoning. When choices are filtered through pre-set templates, the burden of evaluation is lifted. On one hand, this seems efficient: fewer irrelevant options, more tailored paths. But this efficiency is asymmetric. It benefits the system—its metrics, its retention, its predictive accuracy—often more than the individual. *What's easy to choose becomes what's often chosen,* which becomes what's promoted, which then becomes *normative.* The architecture that began as guidance becomes doctrine by default.

And once doctrine sets in, it's remarkably hard to dislodge. Consider how rare it is to alter your device's default notification settings, or to read terms before accepting cookies, or to scroll beyond the first page of search results. These aren't failures of willpower; they are design outcomes. The interface gently coaxes us toward "normal use," reinforcing what others have done before us. The comfort of consensus displaces the rigour of reflection. *Independent reasoning doesn't vanish overnight—it is outpaced by a more efficient substitute.*

This substitution effect can even distort perceptions of freedom. We feel free because we are choosing. But we rarely interrogate the scaffolding around those choices. A dropdown menu feels democratic until you ask who decided what goes in it—and what was left out. A navigation system feels empowering until you realise it trains you to avoid exploration. What matters most is not whether choices are available, but *whether the architecture invites exploration or simply rewards compliance.* In too many cases, modern design does the latter.

The erosion of independent reasoning is not just a cognitive concern—it has societal implications. Platforms that deliver pre-filtered content (news, recommendations, even people) don't simply inform us; they *condition us.* They train users to make selections without deliberation, to outsource comparison, and to accept authority wrapped in aesthetics. As a result, decisions become derivative. Rather than constructing criteria, users learn to infer them from cues: star ratings, placement, peer reviews, algorithmic labels. *The meaning of a choice is displaced by the signal of what others have chosen.*

This creates a feedback loop where design narrows cognition, and narrowed cognition simplifies design.

Interfaces reward consistency, and users—consciously or not—modify their expectations to match. The radical becomes unfamiliar. The unfamiliar becomes invisible. And in time, the system appears *natural,* not constructed. Its biases become the water we swim in, unremarked and unresisted. The illusion of neutrality is among the most enduring effects of good interface design—and among the most dangerous.

Yet, these architectures could be different. Design is not destiny. Consider tools that deliberately reintroduce friction: systems that slow down decision-making, encourage comparative review, or offer context before action. Wikipedia's edit warnings, Signal's disappearing messages, DuckDuckGo's no-tracking defaults—all introduce design elements that *prioritise informed choice over passive flow.* These are rare exceptions in a design culture driven by conversion rates, but they prove a vital point: *choice architecture can be designed to cultivate agency rather than suppress it.*

The psychological cost of biased architectures becomes more visible when people try to *think outside* them. Users conditioned by simple interfaces often struggle in open-ended environments. Give someone who relies on autocomplete a blank page, and the paralysis is immediate. Offer a research interface with no ranking or filters, and choices overwhelm. The skill of autonomous decision-making—*the ability to navigate ambiguity and formulate original criteria*—atrophies when not exercised. And much of today's technology is built to prevent that exercise.

Ironically, one of the most common defences of modern design is that it offers "too many options"—that people are paralysed by abundance. But this diagnosis ignores the real issue: not quantity, but *structure.* Choice overload is a symptom of poorly architected environments that offer options without frameworks. True cognitive freedom doesn't mean infinite choice; it means *meaningfully differentiated pathways*. It means being able to ask, "Why am I seeing this?"—and getting a real answer.

Moreover, biased architectures rarely admit their own bias. Platforms seldom reveal why certain results are promoted, what variables feed an algorithm, or how defaults are set. This opacity serves commercial interests, but it starves users of epistemic agency—the ability to know *how you know*. The interface becomes a black box. Inputs disappear. Outputs appear. And somewhere in between, *the logic of your choice was decided without your input*. This is not a bug. It is a feature of most predictive systems.

The danger is not that people will make poor choices, but that they will stop making *authentic* ones. Authenticity in decision-making requires struggle, delay, and reflection. It requires *resisting the ease of suggestion* long enough to define the terms of the decision yourself. Architecture that biases toward immediacy deprives us of that resistance. It robs us of our opportunity to form a point of view before one is suggested.

To engage with technology more critically, we must begin to *see* the architecture—its slopes, nudges, and traps. We must develop a kind of interface literacy: the ability to interrogate not just what we're choosing, but how that choice was arranged. This means noticing the invisible: how the order of search results influences trust, how default settings reflect corporate priorities, how friction is removed not for our benefit but for throughput. And it means teaching ourselves—and others—to pause. *To consider, not just accept.*

Choice architecture is powerful precisely because it masquerades as neutral space. But all architecture encodes intention. It reflects decisions about access, attention, and agency. The question is whether those intentions align with the user's flourishing—or merely their retention. As long as we confuse what is presented with what is available, and what is easy with what is right, we will remain governed by structures we did not see, let alone shape.

If autonomy is to be preserved in an age of predictive design, the first step is to restore visibility. Only when users understand the architecture can they begin to navigate it with agency—not as passive inhabitants of someone else's blueprint, but as thinkers capable of asking what lies beyond the default path.

From Intention to Reaction

Open a search engine, and before you finish typing your question, suggestions begin to cascade: "Did you mean..." or

"People also ask...". Watch a video on a streaming service, and the next one auto-queues, chosen not by you but by a relevance algorithm. Spend a moment on a shopping site, and your feed across unrelated platforms will soon reflect what you viewed. These experiences are not glitches or conveniences—they are signals of a deeper shift. *The architecture of digital interaction increasingly bypasses intention and feeds directly into reaction*. And the more predictive these systems become, the less we initiate inquiry—and the more we respond to prompts.

At the heart of this shift is a redefinition of how curiosity operates. Human curiosity, in its unmediated form, is generative. It begins with an internal question, a desire to explore, to bridge gaps in understanding or experience. It's not efficient, often ambiguous, and rarely immediate in its gratification. Predictive systems, by contrast, *reward closure over exploration*. They detect the earliest hint of interest and rush to complete it—offering answers before the question is fully formed, suggesting next steps before reflection can unfold. *This collapses the space where curiosity matures into independent thought.*

The cumulative effect of this design logic is a flattening of cognitive engagement. Predictive interfaces operate on a principle of anticipation: they assume what we're going to want before we know it ourselves. At first glance, this feels like assistance. But over time, it becomes a pattern of substitution—*replacing exploratory effort with algorithmic inference*. The system doesn't just help us; it trains us to wait for help. It recasts our role from agent to client, from seeker to subscriber.

This has consequences that are both neurological and behavioural. Neuroscience research into exploratory learning and decision-making shows that novelty, uncertainty, and delayed feedback stimulate activity in the prefrontal cortex and dopaminergic reward circuits—areas crucial for planning, memory, and adaptive behaviour. But when predictive systems remove uncertainty and shorten the feedback loop, *we habituate to rapid closure*. Our tolerance for ambiguity diminishes. The neural pathways that support deliberate inquiry are bypassed in favour of faster, more reactive circuits. The architecture of our attention is reshaped accordingly.

Social media offers one of the most visible case studies. The original promise of platforms like Facebook or Twitter (now X) was connection and conversation. But over time, feeds became predictive—ranked not chronologically, but algorithmically. Users no longer see what they chose to follow; they see what the system calculates will hold their attention. This subtly transforms posting from expression into optimisation: you learn to write for the algorithm, not your peers. Similarly, scrolling becomes less about catching up and more about receiving stimuli. The user's job is no longer to *seek* but to *react*, as quickly and often as possible.

This reactivity isn't neutral. Predictive systems favour content that maximises engagement, which often correlates with extremity, novelty, or emotional charge. As a result, *we're nudged toward volatility and immediacy rather than coherence or complexity.* Deliberation loses ground to response velocity. And the internal metric for relevance becomes: "Did this get a reaction?" rather than "Did this deepen understanding?" What begins as a technical design choice becomes a psychological filter, reshaping our sense of what is worth noticing.

The same logic is evident in predictive typing and autocomplete tools. These systems are undeniably useful—they reduce keystrokes, accelerate workflows, and eliminate repetition. But they also *constrain expression.* A phrase suggested by autocomplete is, by design, something other people have written. The tool cannot suggest what's original—it can only extrapolate from the aggregate. When writers begin to accept suggestions reflexively, over time they *offload the generative burden of thought.* They write to pattern, not to idea. The machine doesn't just complete sentences; it begins to *frame* them.

Even outside writing, similar mechanisms are spreading. In productivity apps, smart suggestions surface next actions based on prior tasks. In music and film, recommender systems assemble playlists and queues. In search engines, the first screen of results is tailored to your inferred preferences. While each of these examples appears distinct, they share a common trait: *they collapse the need for formulation.* The user no longer defines the goal; the system nudges them toward one that fits a behavioural profile.

Over time, *goals become selections from a menu, not constructions from thought.*

This reorientation from intention to reaction carries implications for education, decision-making, and even civic life. In classrooms, students accustomed to quick-answer systems struggle with open-ended questions or delayed feedback. In workplaces, decision fatigue increases not from overchoice, but from the constant low-grade pressure to respond—emails, pings, dashboards—each prompting immediate action without structured reflection. And in democratic contexts, public discourse becomes shaped by reaction loops: what's trending, what's viral, what's provocatively framed for maximum attention capture.

To understand the structural depth of this shift, we must distinguish between *two modes of attention*: exploratory and reactive. Exploratory attention is self-directed. It scans broadly, tolerates ambiguity, and generates questions. Reactive attention, by contrast, is stimulus-bound. It locks onto cues provided by the environment—alerts, notifications, prompts. The digital ecosystem is overwhelmingly tuned for the latter. Its design incentives optimise for speed, not sensemaking. *As a result, we begin to think in shorter arcs, shorter cycles, shorter forms*.

This compression of cognitive timeframes has downstream effects. When curiosity is replaced by suggestion, *we don't just skip steps—we skip synthesis*. Independent learning, by its nature, involves disorientation: the friction of not knowing, the work of finding relevance, the struggle to articulate.

Predictive systems remove that disorientation but in doing so, *they undercut the conditions for durable understanding*. A learner who clicks through recommended resources may feel informed, but without intention, the information doesn't scaffold. It accumulates without coherence. There is no through-line—only a series of reactions.

Of course, not all predictive systems are harmful. When carefully designed, they can support intention rather than supplant it. A system that waits for the user's goal before suggesting tools is fundamentally different from one that infers goals from past behaviour. Interfaces that *prompt articulation*—"What are you trying to accomplish?"—can encourage metacognition rather than bypass it. The key distinction is whether the system *stimulates thought* or merely anticipates and replaces it.

But current commercial incentives rarely favour this distinction. Predictive systems are evaluated on performance metrics—click-through rates, time on site, conversions—not on whether they preserve cognitive agency. As long as prediction serves retention, not reflection, *systems will evolve toward reaction loops*. The more responsive the environment, the less room there is for generative thought. And the less generative our minds become, the more predictive the systems appear—because we begin to behave predictably.

To reverse this trajectory, we must become stewards of our own intentionality. This means resisting reflexive interaction, reintroducing friction where needed, and consciously cultivating exploratory habits. It means *pausing before clicking*, questioning default suggestions, and carving time for unstructured inquiry. More importantly, it means building environments—both technological and cultural—that reward curiosity over compliance, and *reflection over reaction*.

If predictive systems have taught us anything, it's that convenience is not neutral. It comes with cognitive costs. Systems that remove the labour of choice also remove the learning it fosters. And in doing so, they change what it feels like to be a thinking being. The challenge ahead is not to abandon predictive tools, but to *reclaim our role as originators of thought rather than perpetual reactors to it*. We must rediscover what it means to move with intention—not merely through screens, but through our own minds.

The Cost of Premature Completion

The human mind does not think in straight lines. Thought meanders, contradicts, pauses, revises. It falters before it lands. This halting, recursive motion is not a flaw—it is the very mechanism by which understanding deepens and ideas mature. Yet increasingly, our cognitive environment is designed to intercept this process. Predictive algorithms, autofill tools, and AI-generated suggestions all aim to complete our sentences, finish our searches, and resolve our uncertainties before we've fully encountered them. The result is a pervasive shortcutting of thought—a premature sense of closure that undermines the labour of forming, testing, and refining ideas. *We are nudged into answers before we've asked proper questions.*

Cognition, especially higher-order thinking, depends not on quick resolution but on prolonged engagement. A child struggling to articulate a thought learns not just vocabulary, but structure, inference, and persistence. A writer fumbling with phrasing is not wasting time; they are in the act of clarifying their own position. A researcher constructing a hypothesis is engaging in disciplined doubt, not simply data retrieval. In each case, meaning emerges from effort—not from external completion but from internal wrestling. *The process is formative, not merely instrumental.*

Premature completion short-circuits this process. When autocomplete finishes a sentence, it doesn't merely save keystrokes—it replaces a moment of articulation. When a predictive search fills in your query mid-typing, it doesn't just anticipate need—it steers curiosity into pre-modelled grooves. When algorithmic writing tools suggest entire paragraphs based on a prompt, they do not assist cognition so much as *supplant it*. These systems are trained on existing patterns. They generate what is probable, not what is original. And as users increasingly accept these interventions, *they begin to internalise completion as a cognitive default rather than a deliberate act*.

The psychology of this shift is subtle but significant. Consider the concept of "closure" in cognitive science. Humans are naturally inclined to seek completion; unfinished patterns generate discomfort, a phenomenon known as the Zeigarnik effect. Predictive tools exploit this bias. They offer tidy closure—syntactic, semantic, procedural—before the user has truly grappled with ambiguity. This feels efficient, even satisfying. But it trains the mind to avoid the discomfort of incompletion, *replacing productive struggle with passive resolution*. Over time, this lowers tolerance for ambiguity, complexity, and slow-forming ideas.

The educational implications are already visible. In classrooms where AI tools are readily available, students increasingly outsource not just fact-finding but synthesis. A prompt fed into a text generator returns an essay draft within seconds—grammatical, coherent, plausible. But coherence is not understanding. The student has bypassed the intellectual friction of building an argument, weighing evidence, or encountering contradiction. *They are turning in answers without constructing questions*. What appears as efficiency is, in fact, an erosion of cognitive resilience.

In professional settings, the same pattern unfolds under different labels. Smart email tools draft responses. Scheduling assistants eliminate negotiation. Predictive analytics forecast decisions. Each tool has utility, but their cumulative effect is to deskill. Workers begin to follow system cues rather than navigate ambiguity. Decisions feel less owned, more inferred. The space for initiative, dissent, or genuine creativity is narrowed—not through coercion, but through seamless convenience. *The work becomes a flow of completions, not a process of deliberation.*

To understand why this matters, we must recognise that thinking is not simply a means to an end. It is a mode of being. To wrestle with a problem, to sit with uncertainty, to draft and redraft a sentence—these are not just ways of producing output. They are *how we know what we think*. A premature answer doesn't just skip a step; it distorts the shape of the question. It interrupts the reflective cycle that turns data into knowledge, knowledge into insight. *It trains us to prefer resolution over rigour.*

Philosophers from Aristotle to Arendt have argued that thought is inherently dialogical—an internal conversation, a grappling between self and world. Predictive systems collapse that conversation into monologue. They feed us completions not based on engagement but on extrapolation from collective data. This is not dialogue; it is statistical echo. The danger is not simply that we rely on these systems, but that we begin to internalise their logic. *We think in templates. We finish prematurely because we expect ideas to arrive pre-packaged.*

Consider how this manifests in creative work. A novelist used to dwell in drafts—plot lines rearranged, characters revised, prose refined through obsessive attention. Now, story generators offer outlines, name suggestions, dialogue snippets. This may help overcome blocks, but it also conditions the writer to *accept rather than invent*. Over time, the impulse to persist through a difficult narrative problem atrophies. The same applies to design, to coding, to music composition—any field where creativity is iterative. Tools that offer premature completion remove the very tension from which originality emerges.

This is not an argument against assistance. Cognitive scaffolding—when appropriately designed—can extend capacity without replacing agency. A calculator does not prevent mathematical understanding; it frees working memory for higher functions. A spell-checker doesn't undermine literacy; it supports error correction. But predictive completion operates differently. *It presumes the user's intention before it has formed.* It doesn't wait for the thinker; it offers a solution in lieu of the question. In doing so, it *flattens the space where ideas might have taken shape.*

Moreover, there is an epistemic risk in automated completion: *we begin to confuse plausibility with validity.* A suggested phrase may sound correct, but has the thinker actually vetted it? A generated paragraph may flow smoothly, but does it reflect a defensible argument? Completion tools prioritise fluency over rigour. They simulate coherence, but coherence without context is a form of mimicry. The mind, accustomed to accepting what is offered, stops interrogating what it receives.

There is also a social cost. When we rely on systems to finish our thoughts, *we outsource the responsibility of clarity.* This affects not only our own cognition, but how we communicate with others. Language becomes standardised, predictable, drained of nuance. Debate becomes fragile, since positions are less grounded in considered belief than in assembled phrases. *We stop negotiating meaning because we stop forming meaning ourselves.*

The irony is that these tools emerged in the name of productivity, yet their long-term effect may be a decline in the very forms of labour that make thinking valuable: formulation, iteration, doubt. Productivity without process is a shallow gain. It accelerates completion while displacing comprehension. In a culture of constant output, the ability to dwell in ambiguity becomes not just rare, but subversive. *To resist premature completion is, in a sense, to reclaim one's right to think slowly, to think well.*

There are ways to resist. We can pause before accepting suggestions. We can turn off autocomplete in writing environments. We can deliberately embrace incomplete prompts, unfinished thoughts, ideas that don't yet resolve. Educators can assign work that values process over product—requiring drafts, peer feedback, reflective annotations. Designers can build systems that offer scaffolding, not answers—tools that ask before they tell. Organisations can reward depth over speed, original framing over rapid response.

Most importantly, we must shift how we define completion itself. A thought is not complete because it has a full stop. It is complete when it has been tested—against evidence, against alternatives, against time. *To form an idea is to take ownership of it; to refine it is to make it resilient.* Predictive systems offer none of this. They offer speed, not sovereignty.

In the end, the cost of premature completion is not just intellectual—it is existential. *When we stop forming thoughts for ourselves, we lose touch with the very act of thinking*. We begin to live in the completions of others—aggregated, predicted, optimised. The challenge is not to reject assistance, but to *reclaim process*. To value the slow arc of thought. To resist the urge for premature resolution. And to remember that every worthwhile idea was once a problem unsolved.

Chapter 4
The Quiet Decline of Memory

We are forgetting more than we realise, and the loss is largely invisible. In an age brimming with prompts, notifications, search engines, and cloud backups, memory is no longer exercised; it is delegated as a matter of course. Retrieving a name, recalling a number, keeping track of time or place—once mental tasks requiring effort—are now quietly handled by our devices. Calendars remember appointments, browsers recall histories, phones note anniversaries. And yet, as these tools sharpen, our minds soften. The capacity to retain, reconstruct, and reflect—the very scaffolding of human memory—erodes behind screens that appear to do it all for us.

This decline is structural, not incidental. Cognitive offloading—entrusting mental operations to external systems—is as old as writing itself. But today it occurs at a scale and subtlety previously unimaginable. We no longer choose consciously to delegate memory; we do so reflexively. In that reflex, we surrender more than information: we surrender the architecture of memory itself, its capacity for generative thought, its very strain that fuels understanding.

Memory is active, not passive. It links past with present, experience with action, self with narrative. Recall engages complex neural networks, binds disparate elements, and sparks creativity. Recognition—the effortless familiarity of seeing a name or image—demands far less. In a world where answers are a swipe away, recognition masquerades as knowledge. We overestimate retention while underestimating what slips away.

The implications reach beyond cognition into identity. Memory anchors continuity, scaffolds decision-making, and enables wisdom. Its diminishment leaves selfhood porous. Creativity suffers, too: ideas are built from remembered fragments, recombined through reflection and analogy. Narrowed memory constrains the canvas for innovation.

Search engines illustrate this tension vividly. They are remarkable cognitive prosthetics—frictionless, immediate, and invisible. Yet, by supplying answers before effort is exerted, they change how we relate to knowledge itself. Instead of wrestling, pausing, or reflecting, we defer. The act of retrieval—proven to strengthen memory—is displaced by instant access. By outsourcing repeatedly, we weaken the neural circuits that underpin recall.

Notifications and reminders follow a similar pattern. Memory relies on cues—temporal, spatial, emotional. External prompts replace these cues with commands: the ping dictates action, bypassing internal deliberation. Reliance builds; we cease to prompt ourselves. Over time, cognitive agency diminishes, unnoticed, while efficiency appears intact.

This dependence feels benign, even rational. Why memorise a password when a manager stores it? Why navigate unaided when GPS is accurate? Why recall birthdays when platforms alert you? Each seems trivial, yet cumulatively they form an ecosystem in which memory is unnecessary for functionality—and when memory is unused, it atrophies. Neural connections prune themselves, networks shrink, and faculties once robust fade.

The stakes extend culturally. Collective memory—traditions, stories, shared identity—has always relied on context, repetition, and communal enactment. Offloading to servers and feeds fragments this process. Memory becomes decontextualised, individualised, algorithmically sorted. Cohesion weakens; meaning frays. Rituals hollow, histories flatten into data points. Forgetting becomes systemic, not accidental.

Emotion, too, is entangled. Memory carries texture, interpretation, and feeling. A photograph may capture a moment, but only memory invests it with significance: its resonance, its lessons, its place in the narrative of self. When we rely on external artefacts to remember, we become spectators of our lives, not stewards.

This chapter confronts this quiet erosion with neither nostalgia nor alarm, but with precise attention. It examines how memory forms, decays, and sustains, and how offloading—though convenient—can weaken the resilience of thought. It distinguishes recall from recognition, showing how the former underpins creativity, judgement, and depth. It considers the societal implications of mechanised memory: what happens to meaning, identity, and history when remembering is delegated.

The goal is not to idealise a pre-digital past. Paper lists and forgotten appointments were hardly flawless. Yet, to navigate the present wisely, we must understand what we trade for convenience. When external memory substitutes for internal effort, we lose not only knowledge but the very capacity to know. In forgetting how to remember, we risk forgetting who we are.

Why We Remember Less Now

The act of remembering was once a defining measure of human intelligence. From oral storytelling traditions to mental arithmetic, societies across history depended on individuals' capacity to carry knowledge in their minds—to recall, reconstruct, retell. Memory was skill, currency, and inheritance. Today, however, that role is being swiftly and subtly outsourced. Search engines, digital calendars, cloud backups, and note-taking apps promise an effortless extension of cognition. But they also displace it. *We are not just forgetting facts—we are forgetting how to remember them.*

Cognitive offloading, a term widely studied in neuroscience and psychology, refers to the process by which we delegate mental tasks to external aids. Writing things down is a classic example. Using a calculator to avoid mental computation is another. But where these forms of offloading were once deliberate—tools used selectively—they are now embedded in daily digital life. We no longer choose to offload memory; we function by doing so. We trust that reminders will alert us, that autocomplete will finish our sentences, that Google will find what we need when we need it. *We engage not in memory formation, but in memory bypassing.*

The consequences of this shift are not neutral. Neurologically, memory is not a passive storehouse of facts.

It is an active, reconstructive system shaped by repetition, retrieval, association, and meaning-making. When we no longer retrieve knowledge actively—when the answer is always available at a keystroke—we fail to engage the mechanisms that strengthen long-term memory. *Ease of access erodes effort of encoding.* Over time, this weakens both the structure and the resilience of our internal memory systems.

Several strands of research support this. A landmark 2011 study by Betsy Sparrow and colleagues at Columbia University demonstrated what they termed the "Google Effect." Participants who believed that information would be saved on a computer were less likely to remember it than those who believed it would be erased. Crucially, they were more likely to remember *where* the information was stored than *what* the information was. This suggests a shift from content retention to location retention—a form of "transactive memory" in which we rely on systems (or people) to know for us. While useful in team contexts, this approach leaves the individual cognitively undernourished.

Memory is also context-dependent. We remember better when information is encoded in a meaningful framework—when it is linked to time, place, emotion, or relevance. Digital interfaces, by contrast, tend to strip away such context. A saved password, an autofilled address, a search history—they offer access, not understanding. They solve the problem but bypass the process. And the process *is* what makes memory durable. *When there is no struggle, there is little retention.*

Moreover, the type of memory being displaced is not simply factual—it is episodic and semantic. Episodic memory refers to personal experiences: when you first met someone, how a conversation unfolded, what route you took last week. Semantic memory refers to general knowledge: understanding concepts, knowing names, recalling facts. Both types are crucial to sense-making and decision-making. And both are now increasingly delegated to devices. Ask yourself: how many phone numbers can you remember without looking? How many past holidays could you narrate without scrolling through photos? *The data may be saved, but the memory is not.*

This erosion is especially concerning when we consider memory's role in critical thinking and creativity. Creativity is not mere novelty—it is the recombination of existing knowledge in new ways. If that knowledge is not actively recalled, if it resides outside the mind, the combinatory space shrinks. Likewise, reasoning and judgment often depend on remembered precedent—what worked, what failed, what surprised us. When we don't remember, we don't compare. When we don't compare, we repeat. And when we repeat unconsciously, *we stop learning.*

Some may argue that externalisation is simply evolution—that human cognition is expanding beyond the skull, distributed across networks and platforms. There is truth in that. External memory is not inherently negative. A library is an external memory system, as is a diary. But what matters is *how* we relate to that system. Are we using it to extend thought, or to replace it? Are we complementing our cognition, or outsourcing it entirely? *When the tool becomes a crutch, the muscle atrophies.*

There is also the illusion of security. The more we externalise memory, the more we assume it will be available on demand. But systems fail. Devices crash. Accounts are hacked. And even when the data is intact, the ability to access, interpret, and use it depends on attention and context. A memory that resides only on a server is not part of our cognitive identity. It cannot influence decisions unless it is recalled. And it cannot be recalled unless it has been *internalised* at some point. A stored thought is not the same as a remembered one.

This trend has implications beyond the individual. Cultural memory—the shared recollection of history, heritage, and experience—depends on collective internalisation. When memories are stored but not shared, accessed but not discussed, they lose their cultural stickiness. Rituals lose their resonance. Storytelling becomes anecdotal, not ancestral. Digital archives may preserve data, but they do not preserve *meaning* unless that data is lived and remembered. *A memory is not simply what is kept—it is what is kept alive.*

To be clear, this is not a call to abandon technology. Few would wish to return to memorising phone directories or street maps. But it is a call to examine our relationship to cognitive effort. Memory, like strength, develops through use. It is not mere recall—it is rehearsal, reflection, reorganisation. These are not functions that apps can perform for us. They require *cognitive presence*, an active engagement with information that turns data into knowledge and knowledge into understanding.

We might begin by noticing the micro-decisions that shape our memory habits. Do we reach for a search engine before thinking through what we already know? Do we trust reminders over attentiveness? Do we scroll for information we once read, rather than trying to recall its core idea? Each of these habits, multiplied across time and users, reshapes the architecture of our minds. *Convenience is not neutral; it rewires us.*

If we are to preserve the power of memory—not just as a skill, but as a source of identity, creativity, and wisdom—we must resist the path of least cognitive resistance. That means rehearsing rather than repeating. Recalling rather than re-Googling. Reflecting rather than reacting. It means treating memory not as a relic of the pre-digital mind, but as a vital foundation of human thought—one that needs not replacement, but reinforcement.

Because memory is not simply about what we remember. It is about *who we become when we do.*

The Externalisation Trap

Memory is not a passive container but an active force that shapes how we think, make decisions, and construct meaning. It is not merely a function of storage but a condition for reasoning. And yet, we increasingly treat it as disposable—a labour better outsourced to digital devices that can index, retrieve, and organise with greater speed and apparent precision than the brain ever could. We are promised liberation from the burdens of remembering, but what is less often acknowledged is the cost of that freedom: *when we offload memory too eagerly, we lose not only information but the intellectual infrastructure that memory supports.*

The phenomenon is deceptively rational. Why should we memorise a phone number, an appointment, or a password when we can store it securely on a device that will never forget? Why strain to recall a fact when it can be surfaced in seconds with a voice command or search query? The appeal is efficiency, but the danger is atrophy. Offloading becomes habitual, and in doing so, it disables the very processes it claims to assist. *What we entrust to the external becomes excluded from internal development.*

At the heart of this shift is the distinction between using tools *to enhance cognition* and using them *to replace it.* Historically, humans have always used external memory systems. Ancient Greeks employed mnemonic devices and oral traditions to transmit knowledge. The invention of writing revolutionised memory by enabling records independent of human recall. But in each case, the goal was not to eliminate memory but to scaffold it—*to extend the mind, not circumvent it.* Today's digital tools often take a different turn. Their aim is not to partner with memory but to relieve us from it altogether.

This relief comes at a psychological cost. Studies in cognitive science have repeatedly shown that the effort involved in retrieving information strengthens neural connections. The *testing effect,* well-documented in educational research, demonstrates that actively recalling information—even unsuccessfully—leads to better long-term retention than passive review. Similarly, *desirable difficulty,* a principle in memory formation, suggests that cognitive effort enhances learning. Offloading memory short-circuits both. When devices remember for us, we skip the effort. And when effort disappears, so does the benefit.

The trap deepens when this offloading produces a false sense of mastery. Knowing that a calendar contains all your commitments can make you feel organised—even if you never review it. Trusting that notes exist somewhere in your cloud gives the illusion that the knowledge is somehow also retained in your mind. It isn't. This illusion of retention often leads to *disengagement,* a subtle but significant loss of attentional investment in the information itself. Why pay attention if it will be archived anyway? Why rehearse if recall is automated?

Psychologist Daniel Wegner coined the term *transactive memory* to describe how groups distribute knowledge across members—one person remembers dates, another handles logistics, and together they form a collective cognitive system. In the digital age, devices have become our transactive partners. But unlike human collaborators, these tools do not challenge us, question us, or prompt us to remember. They simply hold the data, and in doing so, allow our cognitive muscles to go unused. *The relationship is functional, not dialogic. It stores but does not stimulate.*

More critically, the act of remembering is never just about content. Memory involves *attention, association, and meaning*. When we recall something, we re-engage the context in which we learned it—where we were, how we felt, what connections we made. This associative web is essential to the richness and resilience of memory. A digital reminder may jog your awareness, but it will not recreate the matrix of understanding that emerges from lived experience. *Externalisation captures the point but erases the path.*

Consider, too, the moral dimension of memory. Remembering is a way of honouring: names, histories, struggles, lessons. When we outsource memory, we risk trivialising what it represents. There is a difference between consulting a war memorial and remembering a fallen ancestor. The first is informational; the second is relational. *The offloaded memory is efficient, but it is also emotionally sterile.* What makes memory powerful is not that it is accurate, but that it is felt.

This becomes especially visible in educational contexts. Students now often regard memory tasks as archaic—why memorise a poem when it's searchable? Why learn historical timelines when you can pull them up instantly? The answer is not tradition but *cognitive architecture*. The more facts and frameworks you carry in your head, the more agile your reasoning becomes. Thought is not summoned from thin air; it is constructed from remembered content. Remove the content, and the architecture collapses into dependence.

Memory also plays a critical role in personal identity. We are not merely what we know but what we *remember* knowing. Our past experiences—joys, regrets, mistakes, breakthroughs—form the narrative continuity that defines who we are. When we lose memory, we lose not just data, but the coherence of self. Offloading may protect us from forgetting details, but it erodes the *felt ownership* of our life story. What was once internalised becomes a scrollable feed, disjointed and easily dismissed.

The danger here is subtle, which makes it insidious. Most people do not feel memory slipping. They still get their tasks done, still answer questions, still function. But they are increasingly functioning *through* systems rather than *with* their minds. When the system is removed, stress levels spike, confidence plummets, and cognitive flexibility withers. This dependency is not a technical flaw—it is a psychological fragility. *When memory becomes optional, resilience becomes compromised.*

It is worth asking what happens to society at large when memory weakens. Cultures pass down values through stories, rituals, practices—all of which depend on internal memory. If a society relies exclusively on external record-keeping, it may preserve information but lose interpretation. And without interpretation, memory becomes noise: searchable, but meaningless. A remembered story is adapted, discussed, transmitted; a stored one is retrieved and forgotten again.

To resist the externalisation trap does not mean abandoning digital tools. It means using them *strategically*. Write things down not as a crutch but as a way to reinforce mental encoding. Use reminders as supplements, not substitutes. Make deliberate space for rehearsal—mentally revisiting important ideas, testing recall, rephrasing in your own words. Cultivate *intentional retrieval*, not just passive access. Because the goal is not simply to retain information—it is to strengthen the mental processes that make retention possible.

Cognitive resilience, like physical strength, is not the absence of support but the presence of capacity. It emerges from effort, challenge, and continuity. Every time we choose to remember, to recall, to reconstruct, we invest in that resilience. Every time we let the device do it for us, we may gain convenience but lose capability. *The trade-off is not just between remembering and forgetting—it is between growth and dependency.*

Ultimately, the question is not whether we should offload memory. It is whether we want to become the kind of minds that remember less. Because what we carry in our minds does more than inform us. It enables us to think, reason, connect, and care. The mind that remembers is the mind that reflects. And the mind that reflects is the one that remains sovereign—even in a world designed to make remembering unnecessary.

Recall vs. Recognition

A familiar face across a crowded platform. A password that won't come to mind until you've stopped trying. The title of a film you're certain you've seen, yet cannot name. These moments—so ordinary, so widely shared—reveal a quiet but fundamental distinction at the heart of how we think: the difference between *recognising* something and being able to *recall* it. In cognitive science, this distinction isn't merely semantic. It speaks to the architecture of human memory, and, more pressingly, to what is being eroded in a world of frictionless digital access and ever-present cues. *Recognition is effortless but shallow; recall is demanding but generative. Only one of them strengthens the mind.*

Recognition occurs when a stimulus is presented and feels familiar. You don't need to reconstruct where or why you've encountered it—it simply "rings a bell." Recall, by contrast, requires actively retrieving information from memory without an external prompt. It is the difference between spotting the correct answer on a multiple-choice test and generating the answer from scratch. The former tests familiarity; the latter tests true knowledge. *Recognition is often mistaken for understanding. Recall reveals whether understanding is actually present.*

The consequences of this confusion ripple through every domain where cognition matters. In education, students armed with flashcards and apps may feel prepared because they recognise definitions or formulas. But when tested under conditions that demand recall—an essay, a presentation, a discussion—they falter. The material was present in the environment, not in the mind. *Learning that never passes through the gateway of active recall is not learning—it is temporary imprinting.* Teachers know this intuitively, which is why they favour open-ended questions, Socratic dialogue, and low-stakes retrieval practice. These are not pedagogical flourishes. They are mechanisms for transferring information from short-term exposure to long-term competence.

The same dynamic plays out in professional life. A manager may feel they "know" the principles of a strategy book because they skimmed the summary and highlighted a few key ideas. But when they must apply those principles in a meeting or explain them to others, the knowledge evaporates. The information was recognised in context but not encoded through recall. It sat at the edge of their thinking, rather than becoming part of their cognitive toolkit. *What we can retrieve, we can use. What we only recognise, we can't.*

Digital technologies have widened the gap. Search engines, note-taking apps, and autocomplete systems deliver recognition on demand. The information is there—searchable, clickable, tagged. But the very ease of access discourages engagement. If you can always look it up, why store it internally? If the answer will be suggested, why wrestle with the question? This ambient availability breeds a passivity of mind. The capacity for recall is never exercised, and like any unexercised capacity, it atrophies. *Convenience becomes a form of cognitive outsourcing. The more we rely on recognition, the less we cultivate retrieval.*

The psychological impact of this shift is subtle but corrosive. Recall is a generative process. It draws on associations, constructs links between concepts, strengthens neural pathways. When we attempt to remember something, we are not just accessing a static file—we are rebuilding meaning. Recognition, by contrast, leaves the architecture untouched. It is a fleeting moment of alignment between stimulus and trace. It demands no reorganisation, no synthesis. As a result, it builds no resilience. *A mind trained on recognition is a mind that becomes brittle under pressure.*

Decision-making illustrates this vulnerability. Experts in any field—medicine, law, engineering—rely not on their ability to look up information, but on their ability to *retrieve patterns, principles, and precedents* when conditions are complex, ambiguous, or time-constrained. These professionals don't scroll through options; they sense them. That sense is built not through exposure but through effortful recall. The same holds for creativity. Great thinkers don't just know facts—they draw upon layers of remembered insight that interact in unexpected ways. *Creativity, at its core, is recombinatory memory.* If your memory is flat and shallow, so are your creative outputs.

There is also a philosophical dimension. Recall is an act of ownership. When you remember something deliberately, it becomes part of your mental identity. It has been internalised, tested, retrieved, and reshaped in light of experience. It is yours—not because you encountered it, but because you absorbed it. Recognition, by contrast, makes you a spectator. The knowledge exists, but at a distance. It is *available,* not *inhabited.* This distinction may sound abstract, but its implications are personal. *To live in a culture of recognition is to risk becoming a person without intellectual agency.*

These concerns are not arguments for nostalgia. No one is suggesting a return to memorising phonebooks or reciting dates from history. The point is not to reject technology, but to recognise its cognitive consequences. Our tools shape our habits. And when our tools prioritise recognition over recall, our habits follow. We stop rehearsing. We stop testing ourselves. We stop building the very capacities that make deep understanding possible. *The erosion is not dramatic. It is quiet, ambient, continuous.*

So what can be done? The answer lies not in rejecting external memory aids, but in *recalibrating how we use them.* Use flashcards not as crutches but as prompts for open recall. Take notes not to capture everything but to review and reconstruct later. Engage in retrieval practice: test yourself, write from memory, explain aloud. Delay looking something up—try to bring it back first. These strategies are not about discipline for its own sake. They are about *investing in memory as a medium of thought,* not just a container of information.

Consider the implications at scale. A society trained on recognition will be quick to agree but slow to understand. It will mistake visibility for mastery, accessibility for wisdom. It will be full of people who can identify but not explain, who nod but cannot act. In contrast, a society that values recall will produce thinkers, not just searchers. It will foster resilience of mind, adaptability, and the capacity to hold ideas in tension. *Recall is not just a private skill—it is a public good.*

The cognitive sciences are clear on this point. Repeated retrieval not only strengthens memory but transforms it. Each act of recall rewires the information, integrating it with context, perspective, and prior knowledge. This is how expertise is formed—not through passive familiarity but through active reconstruction. The process is inefficient, often uncomfortable, and frequently humbling. But it is also *what thinking feels like*. And thinking, unlike recognising, is what changes us.

In a digital age, the illusion of knowing is easy to maintain. But the difference between recognition and recall is the difference between *having access to knowledge* and *having internalised it*. Only the latter equips us to reason, to create, and to lead. And only the latter is durable. Everything else—no matter how sophisticated, tagged, or searchable—belongs to the world, not to the mind. *To know something is to be able to recall it. Anything less is borrowed competence.*

The path forward is not radical. It is foundational. Teach children to recall before they recognise. Train professionals to retrieve before they consult. Encourage cultures of explanation, not just exposure. Let recall become the standard by which knowledge is judged. Because in the end, it is not enough to see the answer. *You have to be able to bring it forth when nothing prompts you but the question itself.* That is what it means to know. That is what it means to think.

What We Forget When We Outsource

The most dangerous losses are not the ones we notice, but the ones we cease to register. In the age of digital externalisation—where information, reminders, histories, and rituals are stored outside our bodies and minds—what disappears is not simply content, but context. Not data, but depth. When we outsource memory, we also relinquish the cultural and personal scaffolding that gives memory its meaning: our sense of time, narrative, ritual, identity, and lineage. The cost is not measured in bits forgotten but in *patterns no longer formed*—in the mental, emotional, and historical architectures that quietly collapse when we stop holding things in mind.

Human memory is not just a tool for recall. It is the medium through which we construct identity, negotiate meaning, and transmit culture. Cognitive science, anthropology, and philosophy converge on this point: memory is not a vault; it is an active, shaping force. Through memory we *link events, form narratives, retain values, revisit intentions,* and *anchor ourselves in time.* Without it, continuity fractures. In modern life, we increasingly trade this internal coherence for convenience. Cloud-based reminders manage birthdays. Digital calendars track anniversaries. Search engines remember quotes we once knew. Photo apps prompt us with past moments, freeing us from the effort of remembering—but also from the labour of contextualising. *To outsource memory is to unburden the mind, yes—but it is also to dilute its anchoring function.*

One of the subtler casualties of this shift is ritual memory. Rituals—whether religious, civic, or familial—are more than repeated actions. They are embodied scripts that encode collective meaning. Lighting a candle at dusk, preparing a family recipe on a certain holiday, standing for a national anthem—all of these acts serve to *locate the individual within a shared story*. They are memory-in-motion. But as rituals become digitised, abbreviated, or optionalised, their mnemonic function degrades. A family that once passed down oral blessings now forwards a seasonal e-card. A community that once gathered weekly around a sacred object now convenes asynchronously in virtual space. The surface of the ritual may remain, but the deeper mnemonic bonding—the shared timing, the bodily presence, the intergenerational repetition—is lost. *Memory without ritual becomes fragmented; ritual without memory becomes hollow.*

History too is altered in this offloading. In theory, the internet holds more historical material than any library in history. Yet paradoxically, public historical literacy has stagnated. When historical facts are always one search away, they are no longer held, retold, or internalised. We consult rather than remember. As a result, our relationship to the past becomes brittle. We lose the capacity for longitudinal thinking—the ability to situate current events within arcs of continuity and rupture. Political cycles, social conflicts, cultural shifts—all are flattened into immediacy, severed from their genealogies. *When collective memory is outsourced, societies become reactive instead of reflective.* They respond to the present with volatility because they cannot orient themselves in time. Cultural wisdom, once held in minds and sustained through storytelling, becomes a relic—preserved, but not lived.

The consequences are also personal. Life stories, when not actively rehearsed, lose their narrative structure. Memory is what lets us trace where we have been and why it mattered. We remember a mistake not simply to avoid repeating it, but because its recollection reshapes our current choices. When memory is externalised—stored in journals we rarely reread, in photographs we scroll past without reflection—it ceases to function narratively. Events become disjointed. Lives become sequences of activities rather than arcs of development. A generation raised on lifelogging may possess more footage of their past than any before it—but less narrative coherence. They know what they did, but not always who they became. *Autobiographical memory is a construction, not a catalogue. Its strength lies in reflection, not record-keeping.*

Moreover, this externalisation of memory narrows the space for shared meaning. Human conversation, particularly in its richest forms, depends on mutual memory. The capacity to refer to something both parties recall—an event, a book, a quote, a joke—is the foundation of rapport and shared understanding. But if our memories become increasingly private and app-dependent, conversational coherence thins. One person's reference is another's blank slate. A cultural memory gap widens—not due to generational difference, but due to informational silos and offloaded recall. What was once common knowledge becomes individualised metadata. *When we no longer remember together, we can no longer think together.*

Even the act of learning shifts under this logic. Traditional learning was both cognitive and moral: it required patience, struggle, and attention. It trained the learner in disciplines of mind. Today's on-demand access reduces learning to exposure. We read quickly, forget quickly, and reread just enough to maintain surface familiarity. But without the testing and retrieval that embeds knowledge in memory, true learning does not occur. Worse, the illusion of learning persists. People feel informed not because they remember, but because they know they could find it again. *Knowing that you could re-search something is not the same as understanding it. Memory, not access, is the substrate of synthesis.*

This is not a call for memorisation-as-dogma. The point is not to reject technology or to pine for pre-digital methods of knowledge retention. It is to recognise what is being displaced when we default to external storage. *Memory is not a bottleneck to efficiency—it is a foundation of depth.* It is what allows us to connect ideas across domains, to compare past and present, to carry wisdom forward without having to rediscover it anew. Offloading memory may increase surface capacity, but it decreases depth of processing. It extends reach while thinning coherence. It multiplies options while diminishing anchoring.

There is also the issue of *resilience*. A mind trained to remember—to hold things, to connect things, to build mental structures—is more robust under stress. It copes better with ambiguity because it can draw on stored analogies, metaphors, and models. A memoryless mind is easily destabilised by novelty. It cannot compare, contextualise, or reflect. It reacts where it should reason. *Cognitive resilience depends on depth, and depth depends on memory.*

At scale, the implications are civilisational. Cultures survive by remembering. Laws, customs, epics, taboos, myths—these are not ornamental but infrastructural. They encode lessons learned at great cost and passed down in durable form. When memory is no longer carried but merely curated—outsourced to repositories, accessible but unpractised—continuity weakens. The present loses its mooring in the past. Innovation becomes harder to steer because its orientation points are missing. *A culture that forgets too easily cannot deliberate. It can only improvise.*

The question, then, is not whether to externalise memory. That ship has sailed. The question is what we preserve *internally,* and why. It is about intentionality. What should remain in the mind—accessible, practiced, shaped by reflection? What memories give shape to self, to history, to shared life? Not everything must be remembered. But *something must be.* Without this core, we risk living in a kind of cognitive presentism—always scrolling forward, never stitching backward. The mind becomes a pass-through space, not a chamber of resonance.

To address this, we must design differently—not just our tools, but our habits. Encourage slow reading, repeated telling, shared remembering. Make space for re-memorisation of values, not just facts. Create rituals that bind individuals to history and to one another. Cultivate environments that reward retrieval, not just recognition. Let schools prize narrative knowledge, not just testable knowledge. Let workplaces reward deep context, not just fast access. Let homes hold stories, not just screenshots.

Because what we forget when we outsource memory is not only information. It is ourselves. And when memory is no longer lived but merely stored, the story collapses—even if all the data is technically still there. The past becomes searchable, but no longer meaningful. The present becomes optimised, but no longer grounded. The future becomes imaginable, but no longer anchored. And in this gap, we lose not just memory but *orientation.*

To remember is to connect. To connect is to care. And to care is to keep culture alive—not in the cloud, but in the mind.

Chapter 5
Smart Homes, Slower Minds

The attraction of the modern smart home is undeniable. Lights shift to align with your circadian rhythm before you even register the change, thermostats anticipate your discomfort and adjust accordingly, and security cameras provide a quiet, reassuring vigilance. Appliances respond to voice commands, and groceries arrive as if foreseeing your next need. There is an almost invisible intelligence pervading domestic life, smoothing friction, predicting desires, and eliminating small inconveniences. Yet beneath this seductive efficiency lies a subtle, often overlooked cognitive cost. As our environments increasingly act on our behalf, what becomes of our own faculties—attention, judgement, initiative, reflection—when the responsibility for countless small decisions is quietly assumed by machines?

To grasp this impact, one must resist the usual narrative that frames smart homes merely as conveniences. Most commentary emphasises ease and efficiency, yet there is a quieter, more consequential transformation underway: the shaping of cognition through passive reception. Humans adapt through engagement, through friction. Every minor choice—when to open a window, when to dim lights, how to organise a morning—once required attention and decision-making. Delegating these micro-decisions to sensors or algorithms removes more than effort; it removes the embedded learning. A sliver of daily mental engagement disappears, almost imperceptibly.

Cognitive science provides clarity here. Executive function—the suite of mental skills governing planning, self-regulation, and adaptability—strengthens through exercise, just as muscles do. When a child must remember to close a door quietly, or an adult schedules their own sleep, the prefrontal cortex engages in monitoring, planning, and adjustment. When the environment intervenes automatically, that loop collapses. Spatial awareness, time estimation, and risk assessment quietly diminish, leaving room for cognitive slack to settle.

Advocates of automation often point to the relief from decision fatigue, suggesting that by removing trivial choices, we preserve bandwidth for more significant ones. But this argument is misleading. Not all choices drain cognition equally, and minor decisions, when enacted deliberately, scaffold larger cognitive acts. Consider brewing coffee by hand: tactile memory, motor planning, timing, and often a brief reflective pause are all engaged. Automation delivers consistency but interrupts this rehearsal of autonomy. Convenience, then, sacrifices cognitive practice for immediacy.

The stakes extend beyond cognition to the moral and existential. Our environments shape us not merely by what they permit, but by what they demand. A home that anticipates every action expects nothing of its inhabitants. Frictionless living seems virtuous at first glance—less stress, fewer obstacles—but zero expectation brings zero agency. The home ceases to require engagement or judgement, becoming a passive space rather than an interactive system. Philosophically, this matters. Humans derive meaning from authorship, from actively shaping routines and environments. Lights that illuminate automatically may be efficient, but they are unowned. Flicking a switch intentionally—perhaps marking the start of a reading ritual—carries symbolic weight. Remove enough such moments, and the narrative cohesion of daily life begins to unravel. One becomes, subtly yet profoundly, a peripheral actor in one's own existence.

Behavioural science and philosophy warn against the externalisation of will. When the environment consistently chooses for us, we lose the habit of choosing—not just minor preferences, but responses to discomfort, adaptations to change, and recalibration of routines. Reaction replaces direction. The erosion of intentionality is insidious because it feels like relief: stress diminishes, friction evaporates. Yet gradually, the individual grows less confident in ambiguity, less willing to improvise, more dependent on external cues.

The effects accumulate imperceptibly. Adults reliant on climate sensors may struggle to self-assess comfort; children raised on voice-activated entertainment may show diminished persistence when immediate gratification is unavailable; professionals habituated to automated scheduling may falter under pressure when prioritisation is required. These are not catastrophic failures, merely incremental diminutions of competence, often unnoticed until self-reliance is demanded.

A deeper, existential question emerges: what is the purpose of a home? Should it perform tasks for us, or cultivate engagement, autonomy, and growth? The current vision of smart living leans toward the former, casting the human as a consumer of services rather than a participant in daily ritual. Yet meaningful life is composed of mindful action, situated in time and place, enacted with care. Over-automation erodes the symbolic thresholds that structure transitions—from work to rest, from solitude to social connection, from alertness to reflection. Remove these cues, and days blur; strip away rituals, and experience flattens.

The challenge is not wholesale rejection of technology but discerning use. Which routines should be automated, and which retained to sustain cognitive and moral engagement? Where does efficiency enrich life, and where does it hollow out agency? These are not merely engineering questions—they are psychological, philosophical, and cultural ones.

It is conceivable to design smart homes that resist cognitive passivity. Lights could require periodic engagement or intention checks; climate systems might solicit feedback to maintain awareness; scheduling tools could embed reflection moments rather than compress all time. These are not technological limitations, but deliberate choices recognising humans as capacities to cultivate, not liabilities to bypass.

Domestic technology is far from neutral. It subtly nudges attention, agency, and the structure of daily experience. Ignoring these shifts risks inhabiting homes that disengage us from the very practices that render life meaningful. The question is not whether to reject smart systems, but how to preserve the decisions and direction that must remain ours. A home should stimulate, not merely serve. Anything less is a slow drift into passivity, cushioned by comfort—and in that drift, we lose more than initiative: we lose intimacy with the very fabric of everyday life.

Ambient Intelligence and Passive Living

A home that learns your habits and quietly adjusts itself to your preferences may seem like a marvel of technological progress. The heating knows when you're coming home. The lighting softens as the sun sets. The fridge notifies you when you're out of milk, and the vacuum charts its own path through a cluttered room. These conveniences are marketed as intuitive, seamless, and liberating. Yet embedded within their appeal is a cognitive trade-off that remains poorly understood: *when environments adapt so completely to us, how much do we lose the ability—and the need—to adapt to them?*

The core premise of ambient intelligence is that systems should anticipate and respond without explicit instruction. It is a design philosophy rooted in effortlessness: technology should fade into the background, operating invisibly in service of human comfort. But the psychological implications of this shift are far from neutral. In removing friction, ambient systems also remove opportunity—opportunity to notice, to decide, to engage. Over time, such systems recondition the human to expect responsiveness rather than to exercise intentionality. This subtle but pervasive shift reshapes the way we perceive our role in everyday environments. *We stop orienting ourselves and start waiting to be accommodated.*

This is not a matter of nostalgia for analogue living. The concern is not that convenience is undesirable, but that convenience without cognitive participation breeds passivity. Consider the difference between a thermostat you set yourself and one that adjusts automatically based on historical usage. The former invites awareness—of temperature, of seasonal variation, of comfort thresholds. It requires attention, memory, and micro-adjustment. The latter streamlines comfort, but in doing so, *atrophies engagement*. The user becomes a receiver of outcomes, no longer an agent within a dynamic system.

The consequences of such passive conditioning extend beyond domestic comfort. Human cognition is inherently shaped by interaction with environments. The psychologist James J. Gibson's theory of affordances reminds us that our surroundings offer possibilities for action, which we perceive and respond to. When those surroundings become too responsive—when they act pre-emptively—our role in the perceptual loop diminishes. We begin to miss cues, fail to orient ourselves in changing conditions, and lose fluency in managing our own needs. In essence, *we become less adaptable precisely because our environment adapts so well to us*.

Nowhere is this more evident than in the rise of context-aware automation. Smart speakers, geofencing apps, occupancy sensors—these are designed not to be commanded, but to anticipate. They create an illusion of intelligence by mapping patterns and adjusting accordingly. Yet with each predictive gesture, they bypass a user decision. What was once a moment of conscious attention becomes an invisible transaction. Over time, these micro-efficiencies accumulate into a macro pattern: a human who no longer expects to act, only to be acted upon. And like any skill not practised, the capacity for initiative dulls.

The irony is that such environments often reduce rather than expand mental freedom. While marketed as liberating, ambient systems enforce a certain rigidity—a closed loop of learned behaviours. If your lighting, climate, and entertainment adjust to your past patterns, how often are you prompted to experiment, to vary, to disrupt? The convenience of stability can easily become *a constraint on novelty*. The system does not suggest what you haven't done; it automates what you've always done. This creates not just behavioural inertia, but a cognitive one. Novelty requires noticing, assessing, trying. Automated environments quietly disincentivise all three.

One might object that these systems are customisable—that users can override or reprogram them. But this overestimates both the user's motivation and the interface's design. As interaction designer Donald Norman has argued, *the easier it is to let the system decide, the less likely we are to assert control*. Moreover, many smart systems are optimised for invisibility, offering little transparency into their logic. When decisions are buried in opaque algorithms, users lack the context to make informed interventions. The result is a form of learned helplessness—not borne of technical incompetence, but of interface psychology.

This raises a larger philosophical question: what kind of person do ambient systems presuppose and reinforce? The answer is one who seeks comfort, values convenience, and prefers frictionlessness. But this is a narrow vision of human flourishing. It prioritises satisfaction over growth, predictability over resilience. In contrast, traditional homes—though less technologically advanced—demanded more of their inhabitants: attentiveness, coordination, foresight. Tasks like adjusting curtains, managing airflow, securing doors were not just chores; they were cues for presence, responsibility, and rhythm. Their disappearance removes not just labour but *layers of cognitive scaffolding*.

We must also consider the generational impact. Children raised in ambiently intelligent environments may never encounter certain types of friction that once taught self-regulation. If lights adjust themselves, what incentive is there to think about energy use or circadian rhythm? If reminders and prompts arrive automatically, what is the role of working memory? If room ambience aligns perfectly with entertainment preferences, when does one learn to tolerate discomfort or wait for pleasure? *Without thresholds to cross, we do not build the muscles of persistence, flexibility, or self-direction.*

Critically, the passivity induced by ambient intelligence is not confined to domestic settings. It spills over into how individuals engage with workplaces, social environments, and public systems. A person accustomed to environmental anticipation may feel frustration or inertia when asked to navigate ambiguity or initiate solutions. Expectations of seamlessness become defaults. But much of life—especially in complex, unscripted contexts—resists automation. Disruption, negotiation, and adaptation remain core human skills. If these are not practised in the micro-routines of daily living, where will they be rehearsed?

Designers of smart systems are not oblivious to these concerns. Some advocate for "human-in-the-loop" frameworks that preserve agency while delivering support. Others explore "nudging" as a means of gentle correction rather than full automation. But the larger trend remains one of environmental obsequiousness: technologies that flatter our preferences rather than challenge them. What's missing is *a vocabulary of engaged design*—systems that reward curiosity, require interaction, and scaffold rather than replace attention.

This is not a plea to revert to manual living. It is a call for discernment. Ambient intelligence should not be evaluated solely on the basis of what it removes—effort, delay, uncertainty—but on what it enables. *Does it make us more attentive or less? More adaptive or more inert? More aware or more indifferent?* The goal should not be to make environments disappear, but to make them meaningful. Presence is not a default state; it is cultivated through repeated acts of noticing and responding. When environments do everything for us, those acts cease to be necessary—and soon after, they cease to be possible.

There is a fundamental difference between systems that assist and systems that supplant. The former empower; the latter anaesthetise. A thermostat that offers suggestions based on learning but still requires confirmation invites engagement. A thermostat that decides silently and leaves no trace of its logic excludes the user. The same applies across domains: lighting, sound, scheduling, nutrition. *Where ambient intelligence becomes ambient control, human cognition becomes subordinate rather than supported.*

The deeper risk is existential. A person who no longer acts upon their environment is a person gradually dislocated from place, pattern, and purpose. The home becomes a zone of consumption rather than a theatre of agency. Days become smoother but less distinct. Habits become stronger but less examined. And over time, the mind adjusts not to complexity, but to compliance. It expects less of itself because less is ever asked. This is the quiet cost of ambient intelligence: not that we forget how to act, but that we forget *we ever needed to.*

To resist this drift requires more than technical redesign. It requires cultural clarity. We must remember that ease is not the same as enhancement, that responsiveness is not the same as respect. A home that knows us is not necessarily a home that grows us. If we want environments that make us more present, more capable, and more alive, then we must choose systems that treat us not as preferences to be served, but as persons to be sharpened. Only then can ambient intelligence serve as a partner in human development, rather than a quiet architect of passivity.

Effortless Living, Effortless Thinking

A light turns on before you enter the room. The temperature adjusts before you notice you're cold. Groceries reorder themselves. Doors lock, ovens preheat, and blinds descend with quiet precision—all without a single demand on your memory, judgement, or initiative. What once required a moment of thought now vanishes behind seamless automation. This is the age of ambient intelligence, and it arrives with an irresistible promise: relief from effort. Yet the very comfort it provides comes with a subtle price—one that accrues in the mind before it appears in behaviour. As the physical frictions of daily life disappear, so too does something less tangible but far more critical: the cognitive muscle that effort once strengthened.

The human brain, unlike the devices we increasingly rely upon, evolved in a world that rewarded alertness, adaptation, and action. Our executive functions—those higher-order abilities that govern planning, focus, inhibition, and mental flexibility—are not innate givens. They are cultivated, like physical stamina, through repeated exertion. We become decisive by making decisions, attentive by resisting distraction, and creative by working through complexity. To remove the need for such exertion in daily life is not to liberate the mind, but to underuse it. *The automation of routine can quickly become the erosion of resilience.*

This risk is especially acute in domestic environments, where many smart technologies are now embedded by default. At a glance, voice-controlled thermostats and motion-activated lighting appear trivial—conveniences rather than cognitive shifts. Yet their cumulative impact can be profound. When everything around us becomes anticipatory, we cease to anticipate for ourselves. The home, once a place of active maintenance and adaptive engagement, becomes a theatre of passive responsiveness. One becomes not a participant, but a recipient—less the agent of one's surroundings than the audience of them.

Consider, for instance, how a traditional home demanded continuous calibration. You opened windows to read the weather, adjusted curtains with the movement of the sun, checked locks with your own hand. These acts, though small, required observation, memory, timing, and sometimes judgement. They reinforced your attention to context. They tethered you to a sense of sequence and consequence. *Effort, in this way, was not merely a cost—it was a cognitive investment in the environment and in oneself.* When these micro-efforts are absorbed by sensors and scripts, they don't merely save time—they redirect responsibility. And with that redirection, a mental atrophy begins.

The impact is especially concerning when we consider how executive functions relate to broader forms of psychological well-being. Studies have long linked executive capacity with self-regulation, emotional resilience, and the ability to delay gratification—all traits essential to flourishing in work, relationships, and lifelong learning. These capacities are not abstractions; they emerge from daily habits. The cumulative effect of not needing to act, solve, or even remember within one's own space quietly depletes the very faculties we need to manage the world beyond it.

One of the deeper misconceptions about convenience is that it is purely neutral—that by removing friction, we allow space for higher pursuits. But this assumes the mind naturally fills the vacuum left by automation with intentional thought. Often, it doesn't. It defaults instead to consumption. *What displaces effort is rarely reflection; more often, it is passive input.* The time saved by smart systems is usually reabsorbed into screens, not spent in deep work or enriched social contact. The default behaviours that follow from ease are not necessarily better ones. Convenience does not guarantee cultivation.

There is also a critical distinction between *relief from burden* and *reduction of engagement*. Some choices—like automating repetitive manual tasks—free us to focus on creative or strategic efforts. But other forms of automation, especially those that diminish the need to observe, adapt, or choose at all, encroach on the very conditions that make higher-order thinking possible. If a child grows up in a home where light and climate adjust without input, what happens to their intuitive understanding of change, their sense of sequence, their responsiveness to discomfort as a cue for action rather than complaint? If nothing ever needs attending to, what do they learn to attend?

It's tempting to view this as mere nostalgia for a more effortful past. But this is not about moralising manual labour. It's about recognising that the absence of friction in the physical world has consequences in the cognitive one. *Ease, repeated often enough, becomes expectation. Expectation, when not met, becomes frustration. And frustration without training becomes fragility.* We see this increasingly among those raised in highly optimised environments who find themselves unequipped to navigate the unstructured, unpredictable, and unautomated realities of adulthood or the workplace.

Furthermore, the logic of automation—its promise of optimisation and error-reduction—spills easily into domains where ambiguity, exploration, and struggle are not problems but prerequisites. A smart home that always selects the "right" music, temperature, or lighting subtly primes its user to expect optimisation in other arenas: relationships, careers, politics. The messy work of deliberation, compromise, and adaptation begins to feel abnormal—an inconvenience rather than a fundamental mode of human life. *What begins as ambient convenience evolves into ambient intolerance for anything that cannot be pre-set, pre-loaded, or pre-resolved.*

Even design itself plays a role in reinforcing passivity. The interfaces of smart home systems often remove visibility into how things function—lights controlled by routines, thermostats that "learn" preferences, cameras that decide when to alert. The user becomes less a master of the system than a node within it, consulted only when necessary. And while this may seem efficient, it comes at the cost of *transparency,* and with that, *learning*. You cannot understand a system whose choices you do not see. Nor can you improve a process you never initiate.

The irony is that many of the systems that promise mental relief actually inhibit the very qualities that sustain mental strength. To move through a world that responds before you even formulate a request is to inhabit an environment that suppresses volition. And volition—*the act of willing, of initiating, of choosing*—is the foundation of all meaningful agency. To preserve it requires more than nostalgia; it requires active resistance to systems that, however well-intentioned, replace opportunity for thought with the illusion of thinking already done.

There is, of course, a way forward that does not involve rejecting all forms of automation. The question is not whether convenience is bad, but whether we understand its full cost. Smart homes do not have to be mental dead zones. They can be designed—and used—in ways that *amplify rather than atrophy* executive function. This might mean intentionally designing friction back into key routines, offering transparency over default automation, or reintroducing rituals of care and participation that anchor us in attention.

Ultimately, the aim is not to restore effort for its own sake, but to preserve the essential tension between environment and mind that fosters growth. A home that serves us should not supplant us. The highest promise of intelligent environments is not that they do everything for us, but that they support the parts of us we most want to keep—our awareness, our judgement, our capacity to act. *Because if we let go of those, no amount of convenience can truly replace what's lost.*

Decision Fatigue or Decision Avoidance?

The modern mantra of convenience frequently rests on a simple premise: fewer decisions, less stress. Tech marketers and behavioural economists alike have popularised the idea that the brain, like a battery, drains with each choice, however minor. From choosing what to wear in the morning to selecting a music playlist or adjusting the room temperature, we are told that the less we decide, the sharper we'll be for what matters. But what if this logic, seductive as it sounds, is deeply incomplete? What if reducing decisions doesn't just preserve mental energy—it also suppresses growth? *The automation of everyday life, rather than simply relieving cognitive burden, may be creating a subtle but significant atrophy of decision-making muscle.* In replacing decision fatigue with decision avoidance, we may be trading discomfort for decline.

Decision fatigue is real. Studies by Roy Baumeister and colleagues have demonstrated that repeated acts of self-control or decision-making can lead to measurable depletion in mental resources. Judges in Israeli parole courts, for example, were shown to grant fewer paroles as the day wore on—returning to baseline levels after food breaks. It's a striking illustration of cognitive exhaustion shaping outcomes. But in using such findings to justify automation, we often fail to make an essential distinction: *there is a difference between being overburdened by choices and being underexercised by them.* Delegating choices to algorithms might temporarily spare us mental effort, but it also denies us the opportunity to engage the very faculties that underpin judgement, discernment, and growth.

Take the smart home, a setting now saturated with decisionless design. Thermostats adjust autonomously to preferred temperatures. Lights dim according to time of day. Fridges nudge us with reminders to buy more milk. Even doorbells pre-screen social interaction through video and facial recognition. The cognitive load is reduced, yes—but so too is the user's active role. A house that anticipates your needs may sound utopian, but it also curtails the micro-decisions that once sharpened our ability to think, notice, and respond. *Comfort is not always a neutral state—it can quietly erode our need to remain engaged.*

The broader cultural narrative echoes this preference for frictionless life. Recommendation engines propose what to watch, predictive search completes our queries, and apps schedule our meetings without asking. Each of these tools suggests that there is virtue in sparing us from choice. And in some cases—such as reducing administrative overhead—there is merit. But when this principle scales across domains, it flattens the terrain of our agency. *Choices are not just logistical events; they are sites of self-definition.* Avoiding them too readily dilutes the reflective and adaptive qualities of our thinking.

It's worth remembering that not all cognitive strain is pathological. Developmental psychologists and educators alike have long held that challenge fosters growth. Jean Piaget spoke of *disequilibrium*—the mental tension we feel when confronting something unfamiliar—as a key driver of cognitive development. Without resistance, there is no need to refine or recalibrate our mental models. In adult life, decision-making often serves this same purpose: the act of weighing options, reflecting on context, or forecasting consequences *develops our executive function.* When we automate away those very processes, we may feel relief—but also become less fit for novel, uncertain terrain.

Critics might argue that outsourcing trivial decisions—say, picking a playlist or setting the thermostat—frees up bandwidth for deeper thought. This logic parallels Steve Jobs's famously minimalist wardrobe or Barack Obama's preference for routine meals: eliminate minor decisions to focus on major ones. But such examples miss a critical point: *they chose to delegate deliberately*. Their routines were not outsourced to a machine but designed as expressions of discipline and strategic intent. What we see today is something different—an ambient ecosystem making decisions *for* us, often invisibly and pre-emptively. In such cases, the user is not directing attention but being *diverted from it*.

Furthermore, the narrative of decision fatigue can obscure its own context. The overwhelming proliferation of choices in digital environments—what psychologist Barry Schwartz termed "the paradox of choice"—is often the result of design, not necessity. When smart systems remove decision-making without addressing this root cause, they simply mask the symptom. *A better response might be to curate or simplify options with clarity,* rather than erase the act of choice entirely. The ability to choose—especially in a well-defined, meaningful context—is not a burden but a cornerstone of psychological agency.

It is also worth interrogating the ethical architecture of automation. When systems make decisions on our behalf, whose logic governs them? Recommendation algorithms, optimised for engagement or profit, may subtly bias our exposure to information, habits, and routines. What appears as freedom from choice may, in practice, be the imposition of *someone else's* priorities. The fewer choices we see, the easier it is to forget that alternative paths exist. *The illusion of ease often conceals the loss of intentionality.*

There is, of course, nothing inherently wrong with convenience. The problem lies in its uncritical embrace. Decision fatigue is a real constraint—but so too is decision avoidance a real cost. The first invites better design; the second reflects a deeper philosophical error: that struggle is something to be eliminated, not embraced. *Growth, by its nature, involves tension.* Just as muscles strengthen through resistance, cognitive capacities flourish through effortful use. To optimise our lives purely for ease is to misunderstand what it means to live fully.

What's needed, then, is a recalibration—not a rejection—of intelligent systems. Design can support decision-making without replacing it. Tools can scaffold agency without swallowing it. Context-aware notifications, well-designed defaults, and transparent options all strike a balance between overload and neglect. We must learn to ask: does this system help me think, or does it think *instead* of me?

In the end, the most consequential decisions in our lives—whom to trust, what to value, how to act—are not reducible to automation. They require judgment, self-reflection, and the slow work of discernment. When we eliminate the small decisions that prepare us for larger ones, we weaken the very capacity to meet complexity with clarity. And so, the true danger is not that we will make the wrong choice, but that we will cease to notice we are no longer choosing at all.

The Risk of Becoming Peripheral in Our Own Lives

It is possible, even likely, that in designing homes to serve us more attentively, we have begun to step out of the frame. A home that once required maintenance, awareness, and regular acts of stewardship now responds to our presence before we lift a finger. Lights that brighten as we enter. Thermostats that learn our preferences. Refrigerators that monitor their contents and reorder groceries. Security systems that notify us of movement we never noticed. The pitch, always implicit, is seduction by convenience: more time, less effort. But embedded in this architecture of attentiveness is a hidden trade-off—*as environments grow smarter, our role within them contracts*. We shift from authors of our daily rhythms to respondents within a space that no longer requires our participation. The smart home may know us intimately, but it no longer needs us fully present.

Presence, in this context, is not merely physical occupancy. It is a layered form of engagement: attention, intention, and reflection brought to bear on the small rituals and demands of life. Historically, these rituals grounded us—watering plants, adjusting the thermostat, turning off lights, opening windows. They required judgment, timing, embodied memory. A lived home was a site of interaction between person and place. Today, as systems anticipate our needs, we are no longer required to notice them. *When everything happens automatically, nothing calls us to attend.* Over time, this breeds a kind of ambient dislocation—not dramatic or disruptive, but quietly depleting.

Consider how we now interact with light. Where once illumination was a tactile experience—selecting a bulb, flipping a switch, gauging its warmth and reach—it has been abstracted into motion-sensors and routines. Lights respond to movement or time of day, not to deliberate choice. This may seem inconsequential. Yet each small act displaced from intentional control contributes to a broader shift in agency. *What we do without thinking, we eventually stop thinking about altogether.* The user fades into a passive observer of their own environment's decisions. The room knows when you are tired. The house locks itself. The oven preheats in advance of your arrival. All helpful, all efficient—and cumulatively *displacing the need to monitor, recall, or respond.*

This isn't merely a question of nostalgia for manual labour or romanticising inconvenience. Rather, it speaks to a deeper question of *who is doing the living when the living is increasingly handled by the environment*. Cognitive science has long recognised that our environments shape our minds. The theory of embodied cognition holds that thinking is not confined to the brain—it is distributed across our tools, surroundings, and actions. If our tools now think for us, and our surroundings act in our place, then *the brain's participation in daily life is effectively reduced.* The more the system anticipates and executes, the less it requires of us—and the less we expect of ourselves.

The risk is not only cognitive, but also psychological. There is a dignity in action, however routine. Folding laundry, making tea, adjusting the blinds—these acts tether us to time and place. They orient us to season, mood, and rhythm. *To live is to participate in maintenance.* As Sherry Turkle and others have argued, even mundane tasks offer a form of grounding that digital environments erode. When smart systems automate not only function but context, the human is gradually *unseated* from their own habitat. What remains is a kind of ambient residence: a life conducted in parallel with systems, but not meaningfully entangled with them.

Socially, too, this has implications. In smart homes equipped with voice assistants, the dominant mode of interaction becomes command. We speak *at* devices, not with them. The home becomes an interface to be managed, not a space to be inhabited. Interpersonal interactions may also shift: when homes respond instantly and correctly to our needs, we may become less tolerant of the friction that accompanies human imperfection. *People do not operate with algorithmic precision.* A child who forgets to turn off a light, a guest who sets the thermostat differently, a partner who misplaces a remote—these minor irritations once required negotiation and patience. When machines displace those negotiations, they also diminish the daily practice of accommodation.

There are also epistemic consequences. Living within a responsive environment that requires no explanation—only presence—can limit our understanding of how things work. When devices self-diagnose and self-correct, we no longer need to learn their logics. Consider heating systems: older radiators demanded awareness of air pockets, boiler pressure, and the thermodynamics of drafty rooms. Today's systems auto-calibrate. Convenient, yes. But it also means the knowledge of temperature management—once basic domestic literacy—is no longer acquired. *When everything just works, we stop learning why it works.* This hollows out our competence, replacing it with dependence.

None of this implies that smart homes are inherently detrimental. Technology that supports the elderly or disabled, that reduces cognitive load during crisis, or that saves energy intelligently is unequivocally valuable. But *value and cost are not mutually exclusive*. The issue is not that these systems exist, but that we too readily adapt our expectations of ourselves to match their affordances. A home that thinks for us does not merely reduce our cognitive load; it subtly *reframes what we believe it means to be capable, responsible, attentive*. When the lights dim without prompt, we may forget that it was once our job to notice dusk.

And notice is not trivial. It is *the foundation of attentiveness*. A well-functioning mind is not merely reactive; it is sensitive to nuance, alert to pattern, invested in the minor adjustments that mark care. Smart systems, for all their intelligence, lack this moral texture. They do not prioritise, intuit, or err in the ways humans do. When we let them set the tempo of domestic life, we risk flattening the human experience to a series of ambient conveniences. *We become residents of spaces that respond, rather than stewards of spaces that require engagement.*

The deeper philosophical question, then, is one of subjecthood. To be the subject of one's environment is to initiate, adjust, and reflect. To be the object is to be acted upon. As homes become increasingly animated by design, *the line between subject and object blurs*. If our daily environments are so well-managed that we become peripheral to their functioning, we begin to inhabit life rather than enact it. The cost is subtle, but cumulative: a fading from the centre of our own narrative.

Recovering that centrality requires more than resisting automation. It demands rethinking what we want from the spaces we inhabit. Perhaps we need not choose between smartness and presence—but we must *design for participation,* not just efficiency. A home that prompts inquiry, that makes its systems transparent, that invites the user to collaborate rather than simply receive—this is a model worth pursuing. For without conscious engagement, even the most responsive space can become a quiet theatre in which life happens around us, not through us. And *to become peripheral in one's own life is not a technical failure, but a human one.*

Chapter 6
The Illusion of Personalization

Personalisation often masquerades as empowerment. Curated playlists, news feeds tuned to political leanings, shopping interfaces that appear to anticipate our desires—they all promise the flattering illusion of individuality. The idea is enticing: amid the overwhelming tide of data and information, technology "sees" us. It selects, filters, delivers—anticipating wants before we have fully formulated them. Yet this veneer of autonomy conceals a subtle confinement. The more our environments mould themselves to our preferences, the less we encounter the unfamiliar, the challenging, the discordant—and the less we are compelled to develop.

At the core of this transformation lies a computational mirror. Platforms observe clicks, pauses, purchases, and search histories, then feed us more of the same. This is not incidental; it is systemic. The attention economy thrives on engagement, not nuance. Discomfort causes disengagement; discomfort is therefore excised. What remains is a loop of algorithmic flattery: a carefully pruned world amplifying existing inclinations while quietly suppressing elements that might provoke reflection. The result is not a richer perception of reality, but a simulation calibrated to comfort. And like all effective illusions, it feels natural—but it carries cognitive consequences.

Personalisation erodes epistemic friction—the productive resistance we encounter when faced with new ideas, contradictory evidence, or ambiguous signals. Historically, such friction has been formative: it forces us to resolve tension, sharpen distinctions, and refine critical thought. When algorithms pre-empt curiosity—autocompleting queries, pre-selecting content—we are relieved of this essential mental effort. Comfort becomes constraint; mental flexibility, like a muscle, atrophies through disuse.

Consider filter bubbles. A person consuming right-leaning news may, through algorithmic shielding, avoid opposing perspectives. The mechanism is not malicious; it is optimisation. The same pattern extends to entertainment, science, and health information. Over time, one's environment feels comprehensive because contradictions are absent. This is not ignorance in the conventional sense, but a curated absence of counterbalance—a strategic under-informing.

The issue is behavioural as well as informational. When systems consistently provide content aligned with our preferences, the impulse to seek diminishes. Discovery is replaced by passive intake. Where once we wandered bookstores or debated with peers, we now scroll endlessly, each item smoothed to fit our profile. We do not search; we consume. And consumption, unlike inquiry, requires little reflection.

Personalisation can feel like depth, but it rarely is. Algorithms know patterns, not needs. A binge on crime thrillers yields more of the same, not necessarily because it enriches, but because it is predictable. Systems reward consistency, not growth. They measure resonance, not significance. Content becomes familiar, not necessarily meaningful.

Efficiency is seductive. Streamlining choice spares effort and cognitive bandwidth. Yet this relief comes at a subtle cost. Decisions deferred may never become truly exercised. Many of life's most significant intellectual and emotional developments emerge not from ease, but from grappling with ambiguity, contradiction, or novelty.

Self-conception is also affected. The content presented to us often reinforces our past rather than expanding potential. Growth requires rupture—encountering the unfamiliar enough to destabilise existing categories. Personalised systems, optimised to avoid disruption, trap us in curated echo chambers: comforted, affirmed, ossified.

Socially, this has profound consequences. Distinctly personalised information ecosystems fragment shared reality. Debate over common facts gives way to isolated epistemic spaces, each validated internally. This fracture is structural, not merely the result of misinformation campaigns. Hyper-personalised media, by design, prioritises engagement over exposure, reinforcing isolation.

Philosophically, the danger runs deeper. Personalisation replaces open-ended exploration with probabilistic certainty. Exploration requires surprise, serendipity, and the willingness to be wrong. A life fully optimised for preference is pruned of such encounters. Accidental discovery, challenging essays, and human recommendations—these are not distractions; they constitute selfhood.

The concern is not mere exposure to liked content, but the dominance of preference as the sole criterion. Over time, challenging books or unfamiliar perspectives feel difficult, not inherently so, but because we have lost the habit of confronting them. Friction comes to feel like failure, with pedagogical, cultural, and civic implications.

To reclaim the potential of personalisation, its purpose must be rethought. True growth arises from challenge, not comfort. Platforms should provoke, not merely reinforce. Well-designed algorithms might surprise, confuse, or frustrate—stimulating the very faculties personalisation purports to honour. For a mind untested is a mind unexercised.

The seduction lies in its promise of control. Yet control over what we see is not control over who we become. A life filtered for preference alone is a loop, not a journey. To reclaim the dignity of attention, we must resist the allure of being known too well and rediscover the value of the not yet encountered.

Algorithmic Flattery

One of the most seductive features of modern digital life is the sensation of being understood—perfectly, persistently, and with near-clairvoyant precision. Every scroll, swipe, and search appears to train the world to orbit around our preferences. The algorithm listens, learns, and adapts. What arrives in our feed, our recommendations, our inbox, seems custom-fitted: a playlist tailored to our emotional arc, a video surfaced at just the right moment, a news headline that fits our worldview like a glove. *But beneath this seamless curation lies a quiet danger: the illusion of affirmation as understanding, and the steady constriction of thought under the guise of personalisation.* This is not intelligence in service of complexity; it is calculation in service of comfort.

What we call "algorithmic personalisation" is less about who we are and more about what we are likely to engage with. This distinction is foundational. The system does not know our values, our aspirations, or our intellectual edge—it knows what we've clicked on, paused over, hovered near, or half-watched at midnight. From this behavioural exhaust, it constructs a mirror that flatters rather than reflects. *It reinforces the known, repeats the familiar, and suppresses the uncomfortable.* The goal is not growth, but retention.

This feedback loop operates on a logic as elegant as it is insidious: confirmation bias is not a bug; it is a feature. Every time we engage more with content that affirms our preconceptions than with content that challenges them—and the data shows we do—systems are trained to prioritise affirmation. Political views become sharper, not broader. Preferences become narrower, not deeper. Curiosity collapses inward. The algorithm does not argue, contextualise, or provoke. It flatters. And in doing so, it redefines what feels true.

Take the case of news consumption. In earlier media eras, even the most partisan publications were bounded by physical distribution, limited editorial bandwidth, and a somewhat shared informational commons. Now, hyper-personalised news feeds provide each user a bespoke media bubble, crafted not for objectivity or diversity, but for engagement. A person inclined to distrust mainstream science may find themselves awash in sceptical takes, fringe reports, and anti-expert sentiment—not because such views are dominant, but because the algorithm detects affinity and maximises exposure accordingly. *The result is not misinformation in the traditional sense, but hyper-confirmation: a cognitive diet composed almost entirely of one's own biases, reheated and served as insight.*

This phenomenon is not confined to politics. Culture, taste, identity—all become entangled in algorithmic mirroring. Streaming platforms steer viewers toward shows "just like" the ones they've already watched. Shopping sites learn your style and stop showing you what lies beyond it. Music recommendations spiral inward, forming genre cul-de-sacs where the only novelty is more of the same. *Discovery is replaced with refinement; serendipity with repetition.* The imagination contracts, not because options have diminished, but because systems increasingly pre-filter what counts as relevant.

To understand the intellectual cost of this, consider the distinction between exploration and exploitation—a concept drawn from decision theory. Exploration involves seeking new information; exploitation involves leveraging what is already known. Algorithms, by design, optimise for exploitation. They steer users towards predictable satisfaction. Exploration is risky, resource-intensive, and less immediately gratifying. Left to their own logic, these systems become engines of stasis, *rewarding cognitive closure and punishing epistemic openness.*

There is also a psychological dimension to this flattening. Being constantly affirmed—having one's preferences catered to, one's beliefs reflected—produces a subtle emotional high. It feels validating. But this validation is hollow, because it does not stem from understanding. It stems from statistical inference. *The system does not "get" you; it bets on you.* And because it is a system, not a person, it cannot care if those bets limit your intellectual range, entrench your prejudices, or insulate you from complexity.

This is algorithmic flattery in its purest form: predictive modelling that masquerades as insight. It is the recommendation engine that tells you, "You might also like…" not because it thinks you *should,* but because it knows you *will.* It is the ad that chimes at the right time, the headline that taps your bias, the tweet that echoes your outrage. Every success reinforces the pattern. And the more successful the system becomes, the harder it becomes to distinguish personal preference from engineered exposure.

To be clear, not all forms of personalisation are intellectually corrosive. A well-designed system can introduce meaningful contrast—offering a mix of familiar and unfamiliar, easy and difficult, comfortable and provocative. But this requires a different goal: *education, not engagement; enrichment, not exploitation.* Few systems today are built with that goal in mind. Most are designed to keep us watching, clicking, scrolling—not thinking, questioning, or changing.

The long-term effect is a narrowing of mental agility. Users begin to expect that the world will conform to their preferences. When confronted with discordant views or uncurated experiences, they react not with curiosity, but with defensiveness or withdrawal. *Exposure to difference feels jarring because the cognitive palette has been dulled.* When everything we see confirms what we already believe, belief ceases to be an active process and becomes a passive state.

This has broader societal consequences. Public discourse fragments into parallel realities. People talk past one another, each embedded in a feed optimised for their worldview. Dialogue erodes not because people are less intelligent or more tribal, but because *they no longer share even a minimal baseline of contested but common reference points.* Without exposure to disagreement—genuine, thoughtful, and well-contextualised disagreement—the mind loses its capacity for synthesis. Complexity starts to feel like chaos.

This environment also undermines critical thought in subtle ways. When the majority of what we read, watch, or listen to agrees with us, *we become less skilled at distinguishing good arguments from good feelings.* A post that aligns with our beliefs is rated as more credible—even when it lacks evidence. A piece that challenges us is dismissed more readily, even if it is rigorous. The measure of truth shifts from epistemic merit to emotional comfort. This is not intellectual progress. It is regression masquerading as refinement.

What, then, is the antidote? It is not to reject personalisation entirely, nor to pretend that neutral curation is possible in an era of overwhelming information. The challenge is to *design systems that expand our cognitive aperture rather than shrink it.* This means intentional exposure to dissonant views, algorithmic randomness calibrated for serendipity, and media experiences that reward friction, not just flow. It also means cultivating habits of self-curation: deliberately reading outside our domain, seeking sources that disagree, resisting the pull of predictive comfort.

Ultimately, algorithmic flattery is a test of selfhood. Are we willing to be surprised? Are we willing to encounter what we did not already know we wanted? Are we willing to trade the ease of affirmation for the effort of understanding? These are not technical questions. They are moral and philosophical ones. *To outsource our intellectual development to systems optimised for prediction is to mistake convenience for growth.* And in doing so, we risk not only narrowing our perspective, but outsourcing the very act of thinking itself.

Filter Bubbles and Mental Shrinkage

It is possible, today, to go through weeks—perhaps months—without encountering a single meaningful idea that challenges your worldview. Not because the world has grown more uniform, but because it has become more precisely filtered. With every like, view, swipe, and search, you are telling a system who you are—not in the complex, contradictory, evolving sense of the term, but in a reductive, statistically inferable model of digital behaviour. And the system listens. Not to understand you, but to serve you more of the same. *This is not personalisation; it is partitioning.* And the result, over time, is not simply boredom or repetition. It is a constriction of the intellectual imagination—a mental shrinkage that feels natural because it is so seamlessly engineered.

The term "filter bubble," popularised by internet activist and scholar Eli Pariser, describes the algorithmic enclosure that occurs when platforms feed users content aligned with their past behaviours and expressed preferences. While this may feel benign—after all, who doesn't want relevant suggestions?—the long-term effect is epistemic enclosure. We are gradually sealed inside our own ideological taste bubbles. Content that challenges, contradicts, or complicates our thinking is filtered out, not by censorship, but by an efficiency protocol that prioritises engagement over growth. *The internet promised infinite access; algorithms delivered infinite sameness.*

This filtering process does not require malicious intent. It emerges from optimisation logic. Engagement is maximised when users are shown material they are likely to consume, share, or act upon. Dissonance is a liability in this model. So the friction of encountering unfamiliar perspectives, minority opinions, or complex arguments is minimised. Over time, the algorithm learns not only what we enjoy, but what we avoid. It builds a world that feels increasingly coherent—because it has quietly subtracted everything that would make it otherwise.

The cognitive consequence is a dulling of critical faculties. *When exposure to diversity of thought is reduced, the brain becomes less adept at processing complexity, uncertainty, and contradiction.* It loses the ability to weigh competing ideas without collapsing into oversimplification. The muscle of intellectual humility—recognising the limits of one's knowledge, entertaining opposing views—is left unexercised. Instead, belief hardens into certainty, not through deep understanding, but through unchallenged repetition.

The implications for public discourse are profound. Filter bubbles do not merely produce political polarisation; they institutionalise it. On social platforms, users on opposing ideological poles increasingly inhabit separate information ecosystems. They read different news, see different facts, hear different experts. What one group views as common sense, another sees as propaganda. Disagreement becomes not a matter of interpretation, but of mutually exclusive realities. *Dialogue becomes impossible not because people won't listen, but because they no longer speak the same epistemic language.*

Even within a single domain—say, scientific understanding or historical interpretation—filter bubbles reduce nuance. A person researching climate change, for instance, may find themselves nudged towards either climate scepticism or climate alarmism, depending on their past digital activity. Rather than encountering a spectrum of views, from peer-reviewed moderation to activist urgency, they are funnelled into a narrow narrative designed to maximise engagement. *The problem is not just misinformation; it is monoculture.* A diversity of perspectives is collapsed into a curated echo chamber.

There is also a psychological cost. When individuals are shielded from intellectual friction, they become less tolerant of ambiguity. Cognitive rigidity sets in. Disagreement is not treated as a prompt for reflection but as a threat to identity. In such an environment, even mild counterpoints can feel like attacks, and consensus becomes increasingly rare. *The brain, when untrained in cognitive flexibility, treats discomfort not as a growth signal, but as an error.* The result is a culture of offence and retreat, in which intellectual resilience gives way to defensive certitude.

Educationally, this matters. The entire premise of liberal education rests on the notion that exposure to diverse, and sometimes conflicting, ideas is essential for intellectual development. Students learn not only from content, but from contention—from confronting arguments they initially find unpalatable, and learning to assess their merits. Yet when content delivery is hyper-tailored, this foundational premise is undermined. *The curriculum may still be rigorous, but the extracurricular information ecosystem—the digital surround in which students think—becomes narrower and more conformist.*

There are those who argue that filter bubbles are overstated, that individuals have agency and can seek out diversity if they wish. This is true in principle but misleading in practice. The design of most platforms is not neutral; it nudges behaviour. Recommendations, trending topics, search results, all reflect algorithmic priorities, not open access. Yes, users can override the system—but only if they are aware of it, and only if they choose to resist the path of least resistance. *Cognitive diversity, like biodiversity, requires intentional cultivation. Left alone, ecosystems degrade.*

Some platforms have begun experimenting with solutions—injecting randomised or opposing viewpoints, making content provenance more transparent, slowing down the feedback loop. But these efforts remain limited and often superficial. The economic incentive remains tilted toward frictionless affirmation, not curated contrast. *Until business models reward intellectual expansion as much as attention retention, filter bubbles will remain a dominant feature of our informational environment.*

What makes this all the more dangerous is that it often goes unnoticed. A user scrolling through a tailored feed does not experience it as constrained. On the contrary, it feels expansive—precisely because everything aligns with their implicit worldview. This is the paradox of mental shrinkage in the age of information abundance: *we are surrounded by more content than ever, and exposed to fewer ideas.* The world is bigger, but the mind is narrower.

To break this cycle, users must adopt an ethic of intentional exposure. This means actively seeking sources outside their preference loop, following people they disagree with, reading arguments they find uncomfortable. It means resisting the dopamine lure of tailored affirmation and cultivating an appetite for epistemic complexity. It also means demanding better from platforms—more transparent algorithms, more diversity by design, more room for friction and disagreement.

Ultimately, the problem of filter bubbles is not just technical or informational. It is existential. A mind that does not encounter difference is not only less informed—it is less alive. *To think well is to contend with contradiction, to weigh nuance, to revise one's stance in the face of new evidence.* When systems conspire, however unintentionally, to minimise such encounters, they do more than limit our access to content. They diminish our capacity to be fully human.

If we care about cognitive freedom, democratic deliberation, and personal growth, we must treat filter bubbles not as a design flaw to be patched, but as a cultural warning to be heeded. The path to resilience, originality, and mutual understanding begins with a renewed commitment to friction—to intellectual environments that stretch rather than soothe, provoke rather than please. *Without that friction, the mind atrophies. And in the quiet comfort of curated consensus, we lose not just what we disagree with—but the capacity to think at all.*

When the Feed Replaces the World

At no other point in human history has the daily experience of reality been so mediated by a stream of suggestions we did not choose. Before opening our eyes fully in the morning, many of us reach for a screen that shows us what to care about, what to fear, what to watch, and whom to imitate. These feeds—newsfeeds, video feeds, social timelines, notification stacks—do not reflect the world as it is, but as algorithms infer it might most effectively capture and hold our attention. And in that subtle substitution lies a profound reordering of human consciousness. *The feed does not show us the world. It replaces it.*

What once began as a means of curation—designed to sort abundance into relevance—has evolved into a primary interface between self and world. In 2023, the average smartphone user in the UK interacted with their device over 80 times per day. Yet these interactions are rarely spontaneous acts of exploration. They are responses to prompts, nudges, alerts, and autoplaying suggestions—micro-impositions on attention that shape what we see, think, and even feel. Over time, this habituation rewires not just our habits but our sense of reality itself. *The external world becomes secondary, filtered through a lens optimised not for truth or diversity, but for engagement.*

This raises a fundamental question: what happens to inner life—our capacity for reflection, originality, and unmediated perception—when much of our outer life is intermediated by algorithmic feeds? The answer, increasingly supported by cognitive and psychological research, is that these faculties atrophy. People become less comfortable with silence, less patient with ambiguity, and less practiced in initiating their own paths of discovery.

They become passive consumers of synthetic relevance rather than active interpreters of complex reality.

Consider how exploration used to work. A reader wandered through a library shelf, pausing on titles that surprised them. A traveller stumbled upon a local gallery or small bookshop, discovering a new artist. A student read beyond the syllabus out of restless curiosity, forming unexpected links between ideas. Each of these moments was self-initiated and often serendipitous—unpredictable in outcome, but rich in cognitive reward. Today, the logic has flipped: discovery is no longer an act of reaching out, but of being served. "You might also like…" has become the default mode of engagement. And while this produces a frictionless flow of consumption, it does so at the expense of volition.

The psychology behind this shift is subtle but important. Humans are, by design, cognitive misers. We conserve mental effort unless prompted otherwise. Algorithmic feeds exploit this trait by relieving us of the need to choose, compare, and decide. This seems helpful—until we realise that the very faculties being bypassed are the same ones required for independent thought. *The erosion is not just attentional; it is epistemic.* When we cease to select our information inputs deliberately, we risk losing our grip on how we know what we know.

The philosophical stakes are no less significant. Knowledge, traditionally, has been anchored in *embodied experience*—what we see, hear, touch, and live through. Yet increasingly, our perceptions are derived not from lived encounter, but from mediated highlight reels. A forest becomes an Instagram backdrop. A war becomes a trending clip. A political crisis becomes a meme. The real is displaced by the curated, and the curated becomes our proxy for truth. In this context, *the self is no longer the narrator of experience, but the audience of a feed.*

Nowhere is this more evident than in how we form opinions. In the age of the feed, ideas are consumed like entertainment: bite-sized, emotionally charged, context-thin. Reflection is displaced by reaction. We don't sit with complexity; we scroll past it. This dynamic incentivises not just brevity, but polarity—because the feed privileges what provokes. Nuance becomes a liability in a system optimised for immediacy. *Over time, the mind adapts by simplifying its responses, flattening its thoughts, and narrowing its curiosity.*

There are economic forces underpinning this dynamic. Feeds are not neutral tools; they are commercial engines. Their primary goal is not to inform or enlighten but to retain. And retention is maximised when users are kept in a state of low-grade stimulation—a blend of novelty, outrage, and intermittent reward. This is not conspiracy; it is business logic. But the side effect is a kind of existential outsourcing: we begin to rely on systems built to monetise attention to tell us what to attend to. *The cost is not just distraction; it is disorientation.*

Yet the most insidious aspect of the feed is not its content, but its totalising presence. It inserts itself into every idle moment, every waiting room, every pause. In doing so, it colonises spaces once reserved for reflection, daydreaming, or interpersonal interaction. Where we once looked out the window and followed a thought to its strange conclusion, we now fill the silence with other people's content. *The mind, once a site of inward wandering, becomes a staging ground for external stimulus.*

This has deep implications for memory and imagination. Neuroscience tells us that internal reflection—particularly of an open-ended, undirected kind—is critical for consolidating experience into long-term memory. It is also how the brain generates creative insight: by recombining disparate inputs into new patterns. Feeds short-circuit both processes. They bombard us with fragmented novelty while denying the quiet required for integration. *We consume more, and remember less. See more, and understand less.*

Critically, the shift from exploration to curation is not inevitable. It is a choice—albeit one made easier by the ambient design of our digital environments. Platforms could be designed to foster intentional browsing, to slow the pace of input, to reward critical engagement rather than passive scrolling. Some experimental tools are attempting this—interfaces that prompt users to reflect before commenting, feeds that incorporate opposing viewpoints, recommendation systems that favour depth over click-through rate. But such approaches remain marginal.

Reclaiming exploration, then, is not just a technological task but a cultural one. It requires resisting the default of algorithmic convenience and reinstating the value of unstructured, unsupervised discovery. It means teaching children not just how to find information, but how to question the medium through which it arrives. It means making room again—for boredom, for stillness, for tangents that go nowhere. *Because when the feed replaces the world, it also replaces the spaces where meaning is made.*

A healthy cognitive life depends on contrast. Not everything we encounter should confirm our preferences, match our tone, or mirror our interests. The world is not a feed. It is messy, ambiguous, and often uninterested in our comfort. To grow, we must encounter it as it is—not as it is curated. That requires attention, agency, and occasionally the courage to look away from the stream of what's next. In doing so, we may recover something quietly radical: *the ability to shape not just what we consume, but who we become.*

Convenience vs. Discovery

A recommendation engine doesn't care whether you grow. It cares whether you click. And this simple reality lies at the heart of one of the most significant yet least examined dilemmas of the digital age: the tradeoff between *convenience* and *discovery*. Every time we are served something algorithmically tailored to our previous behaviour—be it a video, product, article, or opinion—we gain speed and ease, but often at the cost of serendipity, cognitive flexibility, and self-directed exploration. *Convenience is efficient. Discovery is transformative. But the two do not reliably coexist.*

Personalisation technology thrives on what's familiar. Its core function is to eliminate friction—removing the need to search, to scan, to select. It seeks to anticipate our preferences based on past patterns and deliver content that fits seamlessly into our psychological grooves. But the more accurate the predictions become, the narrower the informational corridor. Over time, we are increasingly surrounded by content, ideas, and perspectives that confirm what we already know, like, or believe. *This is not just confirmation bias—it is confirmation architecture.*

What's sacrificed is the productive discomfort of encountering the new. Historically, human learning has depended on friction. Exposure to unfamiliar viewpoints, unfamiliar sounds, unfamiliar people—these have all been catalysts for intellectual and emotional expansion. They force us to reconsider assumptions, stretch our categories, and tolerate ambiguity. Discovery, by nature, is disorienting before it is enlightening. But in digital environments engineered for seamlessness, that disorientation is filtered out. *If it feels too different, too foreign, too slow—it simply won't be shown.*

The implications of this filtering are profound. The convenience-driven feedback loop creates a user experience in which novelty appears abundant (new headlines, new videos, new notifications) but is actually rare in substance. A person watching YouTube for two hours may feel they've seen a wide variety of content, when in fact they've been travelling in tight circles of stylistic or ideological sameness.

Similarly, a social media user scrolling through personalised timelines may see hundreds of posts from different accounts, but they're all curated through the same lens of personal resonance. *The illusion of diversity masks a deeper intellectual homogeneity.*

This matters not only for individuals but for cultures. When entire populations engage with information ecosystems that prioritise comfort over challenge, intellectual pluralism shrinks. Public discourse loses its sharp edges. Innovation—the kind that arises from cross-pollination of unlike minds—diminishes. Even democratic deliberation suffers. If citizens rarely encounter values or facts that contradict their own, consensus becomes harder and extremism more appealing. The shift from discovery to convenience is not merely aesthetic or experiential—it is civic.

Yet the appeal of convenience is not trivial. In a world of infinite choice, users often feel overwhelmed. Algorithms that reduce that complexity can feel like a lifeline. And in some domains—shopping, travel, logistics—convenience really is the most rational goal. But when this logic migrates into domains of knowledge, identity, and belief, it becomes corrosive. We risk constructing digital echo chambers that appear open but are actually *closed systems of reinforcement.* The brain adapts by ceasing to anticipate challenge. Curiosity contracts. Intellectual metabolism slows.

The consequences are especially pronounced in younger generations whose formative years have been spent immersed in auto-curated environments. Whereas older users may still recall the serendipity of browsing physical bookstores, listening to entire albums, or discovering opposing views in shared media spaces, younger users are often trained to expect frictionless input. Platforms like TikTok don't just respond to attention—they condition it. Swipe by swipe, the user's palette is refined not through experimentation, but through algorithmic inference. *The user becomes a co-author of their own narrowing.*

This is not a Luddite critique. Technology has extraordinary power to expand human capacity—but only when it is used with intentionality. The challenge lies in recognising when systems that promise to serve us are subtly shaping us. Being "served" what we want must not become synonymous with being told what we should want. True discovery often involves initial disinterest, even aversion. It may feel irrelevant, confusing, even boring—until it triggers a connection that expands our world. But personalised systems tend to interpret boredom as a failure of engagement, not the precondition of insight. *What gets suppressed are not just uninteresting things—but unfamiliar gateways.*

Even in leisure, the logic of convenience can erode richness. A music streaming service may learn your taste and auto-generate a playlist you enjoy—but that playlist is unlikely to include sounds that stretch your sonic imagination. A Netflix algorithm may keep you watching—but rarely introduces cinematic traditions or storytelling styles from beyond your consumption history. Comfort becomes the algorithm's currency. And in this transaction, surprise—genuine surprise—is the casualty.

There are, of course, counterexamples. Some platforms have experimented with randomisation features, cross-cultural recommendation tools, and hybrid discovery models that blend popularity with editorial curation. The challenge is scale. These approaches tend not to optimise for the metrics that keep platforms profitable: watch time, click-through rate, session duration. As a result, discovery mechanisms—though valued in principle—are deprioritised in practice. *Convenience, it turns out, is a better business model than curiosity.*

So what can be done? The first step is recognising that *discovery must be designed into our informational environments.* It cannot be assumed. Users must be given tools not just to follow but to diverge—to cross disciplines, genres, ideologies, and cultures. Designers must resist the pressure to eliminate every trace of uncertainty from the interface. Instead of smoothing every edge, platforms should invite exploration, even at the cost of efficiency. Libraries still do this. So do museums. The challenge is to recreate that ethic in digital architecture.

But the larger responsibility may fall on individuals. The more frictionless our media becomes, the more intentional we must be about seeking friction. This could mean setting time aside for reading outside our typical genres, engaging with voices we find uncomfortable, or letting our curiosity guide us rather than our preferences. It might even mean using analogue tools—books, journals, long walks—to reawaken the slow, nonlinear rhythm of self-directed thought. *Because real discovery requires something the algorithm cannot provide: volition.*

The tension between convenience and discovery is not going away. But it must not be surrendered to design defaults. We must ask: when do we want to be served, and when do we want to search? When do we seek confirmation, and when do we risk contradiction? The answers will differ by context—but the asking must remain active. Otherwise, we become not explorers of information but recipients of inference. And in a world where what we see increasingly defines what we think, *that difference is not trivial. It is foundational.*

Chapter 7
The Effort Deficit

There was a time when difficulty was not seen as a flaw to be engineered away. Frustration, struggle, and uncertainty were markers of engagement—evidence that the mind was stretching itself beyond familiar limits. Today, that assumption has been inverted. Across schools, offices, homes, and even leisure spaces, friction is treated as a nuisance to be eliminated. Interfaces are smoothed, lag is minimised, sentences auto-complete, and decisions—sometimes trivial—are delegated to algorithms, all in the name of speed, efficiency, and comfort. Yet beneath this cultural acceleration lies an uncomfortable reality: we are cultivating a widespread aversion to effort, one that undermines not only productivity but cognitive resilience itself.

The decline in effort tolerance is no accident. It is embedded in the logic of the systems that shape our daily lives. Educational platforms promise adaptive learning, calibrating content to a student's perceived ability—never too difficult, never unfamiliar. Consumer products advertise one-touch solutions and zero-configuration convenience. Productivity software promotes "seamless" workflows, ostensibly removing the cognitive labour of planning, coordination, and recall. Even mundane human challenges—navigating a menu, waiting in line, finding directions—have been outsourced to systems designed to eliminate persistence, patience, or problem-solving. In short, the optimisation target is the absence of effort.

And yet, effort is not the enemy of progress; it is its prerequisite. Neuroscience demonstrates that grappling deliberately with challenging material drives neuroplasticity—the brain's formation of new connections and consolidation of learning. Psychology links frustration tolerance to emotional maturity, grit, and adaptive coping. In education, Vygotsky's "zone of proximal development" identifies the space just beyond current mastery as the richest ground for growth. Paradoxically, we now engineer our lives to avoid that very space.

The classroom illustrates the problem vividly. Digital learning environments and intelligent tutoring systems shield students from the discomfort of not knowing. Algorithms adjust difficulty in real time, reducing cognitive overload but also the endurance required to persevere through ambiguity or failure. Autocomplete essays, AI homework assistance, and instant-access summaries further diminish the habit of sustained mental effort. The result is not merely a different mode of learning—it is a generation habituated to avoid intellectual strain. Knowledge may accumulate faster, but the capacity to endure difficulty erodes.

Professional life mirrors the same pattern. The premium on efficiency encourages a low tolerance for delay, complexity, or challenge. A technical glitch in a video call can derail a meeting, not because stakes are high, but because our ambient expectation of frictionless operation is violated. Colleagues who ask probing questions or demand context may be seen as impediments rather than contributors to depth. Workflows are increasingly designed to circumvent negotiation, judgment, and discretion. What vanishes is the discipline of effortful engagement—the ability to navigate difficulty with intention, rather than retreat into convenience.

Domestic life offers its own lessons. Smart homes preemptively adjust lighting, temperature, and music. Voice assistants resolve scheduling conflicts, answer questions, and reorder supplies. Meal kits arrive pre-portioned; vacuum robots eliminate minor chores. These innovations improve comfort, and that is not inherently problematic. Yet they reinforce a subtle truth: the less we are required to act, the less capable we remain. Mental and physical capacities alike atrophy without use.

Cognitive fitness, like its physical counterpart, relies on resistance. Attention, memory, reasoning, and perseverance strengthen through challenge. Just as a sedentary body deteriorates despite compensatory aids, so too does a mind grown dependent on technological scaffolding lose resilience. Algorithms that anticipate thought, interfaces that pre-decide, and systems that remove ambiguity all cushion the intellectual muscles from strain—and strain is precisely what builds strength.

Research in educational psychology confirms this principle. "Desirable difficulties"—methods such as retrieval practice, spaced repetition, and interleaving—demand greater cognitive effort but yield superior long-term retention and understanding. Yet learners frequently opt for methods that feel easier, even when they are less effective. The pattern is telling: effort feels inefficient, even when it is essential.

Emotional resilience follows a similar logic. Frustration tolerance—the ability to remain composed amid obstacles—is a core predictor of adaptability. Environments engineered to minimise friction deprive children and adults of the opportunity to cultivate this skill. A child who never experiences boredom may struggle with creative problem-solving; an adult shielded from discomfort may become less open-minded; teams insulated from disagreement risk groupthink. Friction is not failure; it is developmental fuel.

The implications extend to morality and culture. A society that pathologises difficulty encourages the belief that ease is a right. When comfort is demanded at every turn, discipline, perseverance, and long-term aspiration weaken. Friction is confused with injustice; challenge becomes intolerable. Yet meaningful life—intellectual, professional, and ethical—requires sustained engagement with the difficult, the ambiguous, and the unrewarding. Effort signals values, not merely outcomes.

This chapter does not advocate nostalgia nor reject intelligent tools outright. Its case is for reclaiming effort as a cultivated virtue. Just as athletes train by exertion, we must consider cognitive and emotional challenge as training for modern life. That may mean reading complex texts rather than summaries, learning skills without relying solely on shortcuts, engaging in conversations that demand active listening, tolerating ambiguity, or sitting with boredom rather than reflexively seeking stimulation.

Ultimately, the deficit of effort is a cultural, not merely technical, problem. It reflects the stories we tell ourselves about what constitutes a worthwhile life or work. Designing exclusively for ease risks a world where nothing feels difficult—and very little feels meaningful. Growth, as every mature mind understands, begins precisely where comfort ends.

The Disappearance of Struggle

Struggle, once an implicit part of learning and growth, is being quietly engineered out of modern life. In its place: convenience, acceleration, and ease. Tools that promise efficiency and comfort have proliferated across education, the workplace, and the home—not as accessories, but as central mediators of experience. While these tools have undoubtedly improved access, speed, and user-friendliness, they have also reduced our exposure to productive discomfort, the kind of difficulty that once forged skill, stamina, and insight. *By removing struggle, we may be stripping out the very conditions required for real development.*

In education, the disappearance of struggle is most visible in the shift from active learning to algorithmic instruction. Adaptive learning platforms, once hailed as breakthroughs, are now commonplace: systems that tailor material to a student's current performance, feeding them questions neither too easy nor too hard. On the surface, this reduces boredom and discouragement. But beneath that efficiency lies a hidden cost: the erosion of *productive friction*. The most meaningful learning often occurs not when answers come quickly, but when a student lingers at the edge of confusion—wrestling, revisiting, revising. When we design out that tension, what remains is often surface-level fluency: fast, fluid, and fragile.

Moreover, the digital environment has made it easier to *bypass* learning entirely. A student who once read chapters and annotated margins now watches a three-minute explainer. An aspiring writer can use generative software to produce a grammatically flawless paragraph without ever confronting the hard work of revision. Even in mathematics, tools like Photomath allow students to snap a photo of an equation and receive step-by-step solutions in seconds. *The effort once spent in understanding is redirected toward locating tools to avoid understanding.* This is not learning; it is delegation.

Such delegation does not end in the classroom. In professional settings, the emphasis on "frictionless" workflow and "seamless" interfaces reflects a broader unease with difficulty. Consider how corporate software environments have evolved: once requiring employees to navigate complex menus, troubleshoot bugs, or problem-solve independently, today's systems offer preconfigured dashboards, real-time guidance, and context-aware prompts. The result is a culture of *dependable minimalism,* where workers are expected to act, but not necessarily to understand. The pressure to perform remains, but the invitation to engage deeply has weakened. This breeds not only skill stagnation but fragility in the face of unexpected problems. A professional who has never had to wrestle with a poorly designed system is ill-prepared when the system inevitably fails.

Nowhere is this fragility more evident than in our growing intolerance for process-related delay. People recoil at buffering symbols, abandoned carts due to complex checkouts, and switch services because of minor interface glitches. Yet each of these disruptions was once an ordinary feature of navigating the world—a moment to pause, recalibrate, or troubleshoot. Today, such moments are deemed unacceptable. The expectation is *instantaneous fluency*, not perseverance. And that shift, while subtle, is transformative: it trains us to associate difficulty with dysfunction, rather than growth.

Domestic life is not exempt from this erosion. Voice assistants adjust lighting, answer questions, and reorder groceries, removing small but meaningful acts of engagement. Smart fridges manage expiry dates. Automated lawnmowers keep grass trimmed without sweat or thought. Navigation apps guide us turn-by-turn, leaving us unable to reconstruct routes even after multiple visits. These tools serve real purposes, but their cumulative effect is profound: *they reduce our requirement to struggle—and with it, our capacity to adapt when systems break, contexts shift, or tools are unavailable.*

One might argue this is simply progress—that we are now free to focus on higher-order challenges rather than getting stuck in the mundane. But this presumes that struggle was only ever an obstacle. In fact, *productive struggle is often a crucible for growth.* It is in wrestling with complex instructions that we understand process. In attempting and failing to fix something that we gain mechanical intuition. In drafting and redrafting that we internalise narrative form. Take these efforts away, and what is left is not mastery, but dependency—on systems, shortcuts, and software that know more than we do, and therefore *own more than we do*.

This shift is not merely functional; it is psychological. Repeated exposure to low-effort solutions reshapes our expectations about what life should feel like. Tasks that once demanded attention and preparation now feel burdensome. Learning curves, once accepted as normal, become intolerable. A student encountering their first unfamiliar interface may quickly label it "bad design." A worker faced with a non-intuitive tool may resist rather than adapt. *What disappears is not just comfort with difficulty—but the very expectation that difficulty is part of the process.*

These effects are magnified by the cultural language of ease. We valorise minimalism, speed, and simplification. The most celebrated technologies are those that "just work." A good interface is one that is "invisible." This ethos, while elegant in design, is impoverishing in practice. *When everything feels easy, nothing feels earned.* And what is not earned is rarely understood. What is not understood is easily lost.

There is also an ethical dimension to the disappearance of struggle. When technologies do all the hard parts, the distribution of competence becomes unequal. Those with access to intuitive tools glide ahead. Those without must rely on older methods—or worse, remain excluded. But more subtly, those who never *needed* to struggle often lack appreciation for those who *must*. This erodes not only skill, but empathy. If you have never struggled to navigate bureaucracy, to decode instructions, or to build something from scratch, it is easy to dismiss those who falter as lazy or slow. *Struggle teaches not just competence, but compassion.*

To defend struggle is not to fetishise suffering. Not all struggle is meaningful, and not all difficulty is productive. But the reflex to eliminate challenge rather than navigate it is creating a culture that is increasingly impatient, superficial, and brittle. Consider the contrast between learning a language through daily immersive effort—trial and error, listening, mimicking—and downloading an app that gamifies vocabulary without requiring you to speak aloud. One path builds fluency and confidence; the other builds familiarity with a UI. One is hard-earned and lasting; the other is light-touch and fragile. *We are choosing the second path not because it is better, but because it is easier.*

This shift extends even into how we think about time. Struggle, by its nature, is slow. It resists scheduling. It demands presence. But in environments where every second must yield visible output, where time is money and attention is currency, *slowness becomes a liability*. The consequence is not just personal burnout, but systemic oversimplification. We build policies, curricula, and workflows that assume a straight path—step-by-step, no deviation, no failure. And when reality resists that simplicity, we add more layers of automation rather than pausing to restore the human capacity to work through problems.

If there is a path forward, it does not lie in abandoning our tools. It lies in *reintegrating struggle into our design logic.* Educational platforms should not only adapt to performance, but periodically *exceed it*—pushing learners into discomfort with support, not rescue. Workplaces should value not just speed and polish, but evidence of difficult thinking: dead ends, failed experiments, tough decisions. At home, we might resist the impulse to outsource every inconvenience. Cook from scratch. Read without skimming. Repair rather than replace. These are not nostalgic gestures; they are exercises in agency.

Ultimately, the question is not whether struggle is necessary—we know it is. The question is whether we are willing to *tolerate* it, even invite it, in a world increasingly optimised for its absence. If we are not, the long-term consequences will not be technological. They will be human. We will raise learners who do not persist, workers who do not adapt, citizens who do not engage. And in the absence of effort, we will lose the very traits—curiosity, resilience, ingenuity—that once defined our progress. *What vanishes with struggle is not just hardship, but growth itself.*

Frustration Tolerance as Cognitive Muscle

Frustration has acquired a bad reputation in modern life—an intruder to be eliminated, an inefficiency to be engineered out. Yet frustration, when encountered within meaningful effort, is not merely tolerable—it is essential. Like a muscle taxed through resistance, the human mind strengthens through grappling with friction. *To remove frustration from our environments is to remove the very substance through which grit, adaptability, and creative breakthroughs are forged.* And increasingly, that is precisely what we are doing.

Contemporary technologies and systems, in their pursuit of seamlessness, aim to intercept frustration before it arises. Autocomplete spares us the effort of completing our own thoughts. Predictive search refines our inquiries before we have fully formed them. Navigation apps reroute us instantly at the first sign of delay. While these innovations increase speed and efficiency, they also quietly short-circuit cognitive processes that require us to confront discomfort—uncertainty, ambiguity, and complexity. The cumulative result is a populace less practised in sitting with challenge, less equipped to navigate disruption, and less patient in the face of incomplete resolution.

This loss is not accidental. It is a by-product of design incentives. In product development, a "frustration-free" user experience is the holy grail. Usability testing revolves around reducing moments of delay, confusion, or indecision. Every menu option, every prompt, every micro-interaction is optimised to minimise cognitive demand. And for good reason: users gravitate toward tools that anticipate rather than challenge them. But *what serves the bottom line of a product may erode the backbone of a mind.* When the only acceptable interface is one that requires no learning curve, we gradually train ourselves to equate effort with failure.

The implications extend beyond technology. In educational contexts, frustration is increasingly framed as a barrier to learning, rather than a precondition for it. Curriculum designers speak of "optimising engagement" by reducing "cognitive overload"—a term that too often conflates difficulty with dysfunction. The push for gamification, bite-sized content, and instant feedback may improve short-term motivation, but it can also devalue the very skills that matter most: delayed gratification, strategic perseverance, and emotional regulation under strain. A student who has never had to wrestle with an intractable problem is not a well-supported learner—they are an undertrained thinker. *Frustration tolerance is not an obstacle to learning; it is a form of learning.*

In psychology, frustration tolerance refers to the ability to withstand uncomfortable feelings when goals are obstructed. It is one of the foundational elements of resilience. Children who build this capacity early—through difficult puzzles, social negotiation, or physical tasks—show greater adaptability later in life. Adults who retain it are more likely to persist through ambiguity, absorb failure constructively, and innovate when strategies falter. In this light, frustration is not an irritant to be managed, but *a metabolic demand necessary for psychological development.* When life gets too easy, minds grow too soft.

Compare the experience of solving a complex problem alone versus being walked through a tutorial. The former requires trial and error, the reorganisation of assumptions, and internal self-regulation. The latter is efficient but shallow. It removes the discomfort—and with it, the opportunity to build mental stamina. In a world increasingly structured around immediate answers, *we are outsourcing the very conditions that build cognitive fitness.* The more our tools remove friction, the more friction surprises us when it reappears in life.

We see this erosion of frustration tolerance in workplaces too, especially in younger professionals entering the labour market with little exposure to protracted challenge. Managers now report a rise in what has been dubbed "fragility fatigue"—the growing burden of managing employees who interpret setbacks not as growth signals, but as threats to self-worth. When feedback, ambiguity, or slow progress are met with anxiety rather than resilience, *the organisation becomes less adaptive, less robust, and ultimately less innovative.* Without the grit to persist through early-stage complexity, creative thinking short-circuits into premature conclusions or avoidance behaviours.

Innovation itself depends on a sustained relationship with frustration. Scientific discovery, artistic expression, entrepreneurial experimentation—all require a willingness to sit with uncertainty, failure, and stuckness. The eureka moment, contrary to popular myth, is not a sudden spark but the culmination of extended cognitive labour under constraint. Frustration is not the thing that blocks creativity; it is the crucible in which creativity is formed. Remove it too early, and what remains is mimicry without insight.

This is not a call to reintroduce suffering for its own sake. Not all frustration is constructive. Chronic, purposeless friction—whether from broken systems, poorly designed interfaces, or unjust hierarchies—should be eliminated. But the current pendulum has swung too far in the opposite direction. *We now mistake any discomfort for dysfunction, any pause for failure, any confusion for danger.* In doing so, we lose the chance to build the capacities that only discomfort can provoke.

The analogy to physical training is instructive. Just as muscles require resistance to grow, minds require difficulty to adapt. A workout that never challenges the body will never strengthen it. Likewise, a learning or working experience that never frustrates will never develop grit. The bodybuilder understands that fatigue is not a sign to stop, but a signal of growth underway. So too with the mind. The key is not to avoid frustration, but to interpret it correctly: not as a sign that something is wrong, but as a signal that something important is happening.

Yet culturally, we have begun to pathologise this signal. When a student grows frustrated, we change the task. When a worker becomes overwhelmed, we lower the bar. When a user complains, we simplify the tool. All of these adjustments may have short-term benefits—but they also carry long-term costs. *The erosion of frustration tolerance is not simply an emotional shift; it is a cognitive reprogramming.* We are building habits of mind that expect ease, demand immediacy, and recoil from ambiguity. These are not the habits from which breakthroughs emerge.

There is a generational dimension to this shift as well. Younger generations, shaped by environments of instant gratification, are often cast as "less resilient." But such judgements risk blaming individuals for systemic patterns. When every interface, every educational tool, every social platform has been optimised to eliminate challenge, *it is hardly surprising that users become less tolerant of friction.* The solution lies not in moralising, but in rebuilding friction into our cultural architecture—in measured, intentional ways.

Designing for frustration tolerance does not mean creating frustrating systems. It means designing for challenge. It means rewarding persistence rather than speed, celebrating iteration over instant success, and teaching learners how to re-engage after failure rather than sidestepping it entirely. It means restoring the expectation that worthwhile outcomes require discomfort—that struggle is not a detour, but the path itself.

Ultimately, the stakes are high. A society that cannot tolerate frustration is a society that cannot innovate under pressure, cannot educate for endurance, and cannot adapt to the unknown. It becomes brittle, reactive, and dependent—on automation, on simplification, on externally supplied certainty. To reverse this trend, we must reframe our relationship to discomfort. We must treat frustration not as a glitch in the system, but as an invitation to grow. *Frustration tolerance is not just a skill—it is a civic virtue, a developmental necessity, and a cultural imperative.*

To build it, we must welcome friction where it matters. Let students get stuck, then help them find their way. Let workers confront ambiguity, then equip them to navigate it. Let systems challenge users, then reward effort, not just outcome. In doing so, we will not only restore a lost skill—we will restore the foundation of meaningful learning, durable creativity, and genuine progress. The future belongs not to those who are most protected from frustration, but to those most capable of metabolising it.

Mental Endurance and Atrophy

Endurance, in its truest form, is not merely the capacity to persist, but the ability to do so *with integrity of attention and coherence of thought over time.* In the physical domain, we understand that muscles weaken when not used, that cardiovascular health declines without sustained effort, and that agility is lost through neglect. What is less widely appreciated—but no less true—is that the same principle applies to the mind. Cognitive stamina, like muscular strength, is built through regular exertion and depleted through habitual avoidance. *The brain does not automatically preserve its sharpness; it must be taxed, stretched, and fatigued to retain its fitness.*

Modern environments, however, are engineered in the opposite direction. Much of contemporary life is designed to reduce cognitive strain. Tasks that once required sustained attention, delayed gratification, and memory recall are now increasingly mediated by convenience tools—algorithms that finish our sentences, notifications that pre-empt our intentions, and interfaces that smooth over ambiguity. While these tools offer undeniable gains in efficiency, they also *unintentionally rob us of the very friction through which mental endurance is built.* Without that friction, the mind becomes prone to distraction, intolerant of ambiguity, and prematurely fatigued by complexity.

The physiological analogy is more than metaphor. Neuroscience confirms that effortful cognitive engagement recruits and strengthens specific neural circuits, particularly within the prefrontal cortex—the seat of executive function, attention control, and decision-making. Repeated engagement of these circuits leads to neuroplastic adaptations that enhance focus, working memory, and self-regulation. Just as lifting weights increases the capacity of muscle fibres, *engaging with sustained mental effort thickens and connects neural networks that support higher-order reasoning.* But like any training regimen, the benefits are reversible. Prolonged disuse leads to a measurable decline in function.

One does not need to look far to see the symptoms of mental atrophy. Professionals report a diminishing capacity for deep work—defined by Cal Newport as the ability to concentrate on cognitively demanding tasks without distraction. Students increasingly struggle with tasks requiring sustained reading or complex problem-solving. Even recreational attention has shifted—books are abandoned for short-form video, conversation for message threads, curiosity for pre-curated feeds. These are not merely lifestyle preferences; they are reflections of *a systemic drift away from cognitively effortful engagement.* And the drift has consequences.

Mental atrophy is rarely sudden. It manifests incrementally—first as a preference for speed over depth, then as discomfort with complexity, and finally as avoidance of sustained thinking altogether. Tasks that once required modest attention now feel disproportionately draining. Ambiguity feels threatening rather than interesting. Problem-solving begins to rely more on heuristic shortcuts than careful analysis. The capacity for cognitive endurance shrinks, not because of age or intelligence, but from underuse.

Critically, this is not a generational problem but a design problem. The environments we inhabit—workplaces, classrooms, digital platforms—have become optimised for immediacy and ease. Interfaces anticipate our next move before we've formulated it. Educational platforms offer adaptive content that matches our current level rather than pushing us beyond it. Productivity apps segment tasks into micro-goals to maintain momentum but often remove the need to structure one's own time or thinking. *Each of these changes feels helpful in isolation, but cumulatively, they recondition us to expect low-effort engagement.* Mental fatigue arrives more quickly because the mind has been conditioned to work in short, shallow bursts.

There is also a cultural dimension to this atrophy. In many sectors, the currency of productivity has shifted from depth to output volume. The premium is placed on responsiveness rather than reflection, multitasking rather than mastery. Emails answered, tabs open, meetings attended—these become the new proxies for mental work. But they demand *attention residue,* not sustained application. Over time, they deplete the mind's baseline ability to endure silence, concentrate deeply, or grapple with unresolved ideas. *Mental endurance thrives on undivided attention. Yet modern work splits it into fragments too small to yield intellectual nutrition.*

It would be a mistake, however, to frame this solely as a lament for a lost past. The real challenge is not nostalgia for analogue focus, but *a forward-looking recognition that mental endurance must be deliberately preserved in a world that no longer rewards it by default.* If physical fitness now requires intentional training to counteract sedentary habits, so too does cognitive fitness require deliberate effort to counteract informational ease. The brain, like the body, must be exercised beyond comfort to maintain capacity.

Such training is rarely glamorous. It requires extended reading without interruption. Writing and thinking in drafts, not tweets. Wrestling with ideas that resist resolution. Committing to work that will not yield immediate results. None of these practices are efficient in the modern sense—but *efficiency is not the goal of cognitive training; stamina is.* And stamina grows only when the brain is placed under tension that it must adapt to bear.

There is, of course, a paradox at the heart of this discussion. The very tools that enable our intellectual reach also contribute to its contraction. A researcher may have access to millions of academic papers, but never read a full one. A designer may wield powerful creative software, but use only templated shortcuts. A policymaker may receive real-time analytics, but have little time to consider the slow consequences of structural decisions. The problem is not the tool, but the pattern of use. *When tools replace the need for effort rather than amplify it, the mind's capacity to endure weakens quietly over time.*

This is not to suggest that mental endurance is incompatible with modern life. On the contrary, the demands of contemporary complexity require it more than ever. But meeting those demands requires a cultural shift in how we value and cultivate deep thinking. It means redesigning work to include blocks of protected focus, not just sprints of reactive tasking. It means structuring education not just for mastery, but for discomfort tolerance. It means treating mental fatigue not as a failure, but as a sign that genuine work is occurring.

And it means accepting that *mental strength is not something we inherit—it is something we train.* Like physical stamina, it cannot be delegated, downloaded, or delivered. It must be built internally, through acts of sustained attention, constructive struggle, and chosen discomfort. The human brain remains capable of extraordinary endurance—but only when we choose to use it in ways that stretch rather than spare it.

If we fail to cultivate this capacity, the risks are not merely personal. At the societal level, cognitive atrophy diminishes our ability to respond to complexity, nuance, and long-term consequence. It encourages a politics of slogans, a science of shortcuts, and a culture of reaction. It weakens our collective ability to plan, to deliberate, to solve systemic problems that cannot be addressed through quick fixes or clever hacks. *Mental endurance is not simply a private virtue—it is a public necessity.*

Rebuilding it starts small. Choosing the longer route in thought rather than the immediate one. Reading the original source, not the summary. Sitting with a difficult idea before moving on. Practising attention as a discipline, not just a resource. These are not grand gestures, but cumulative ones. And they matter. Because in the end, the mind, like the body, becomes what it repeatedly does. Use it, and it strengthens. Spare it, and it fades. The choice is ongoing, and so is the consequence.

Rebuilding Cognitive Stamina

There is a particular kind of mental energy that modern life increasingly neglects: the quiet, often uncelebrated capacity to persist with concentration across extended periods of discomfort. Not the thrill of short bursts of inspiration, but the disciplined return to complex thought after interruption; not the productivity hacks that shave seconds off tasks, but the hard-earned ability to engage with what does not yield immediate reward. This is cognitive stamina—the sustained effort required for reflective problem-solving, enduring ambiguity, navigating complexity, and integrating competing ideas. It is not a trait we're born with, but a capacity developed through practice. And it is eroding in the very environments we celebrate as cognitively 'optimised'.

The modern toolkit—rich in digital efficiency, convenience, and low-friction interaction—has steadily reduced the presence of deliberate struggle in daily life. Algorithms anticipate what we seek before we finish typing. Workflows are modularised into pre-defined steps. Learning is gamified, feedback instant, and challenge smoothed into digestible increments. All of this is intended to make things easier. And it does. But *easy* is not neutral. *Easy, when made habitual, becomes a cognitive default—eroding the brain's tolerance for what is hard, slow, or unresolved.* When every action requires less thought, attention, and persistence, the skill of thinking deeply for long stretches atrophies—not due to lack of intellect, but from lack of training.

Rebuilding this stamina requires a reversal of that default. It demands friction—not of the frustrating, bureaucratic kind, but *intentional friction that restores the role of sustained effort in how we think, learn, and live.* Just as we do not expect physical endurance to improve without exertion, we must stop assuming cognitive resilience will develop in comfort. Attention, memory, emotional regulation, decision-making—these are not static faculties but muscles that must be worked against resistance to retain strength. The path to re-strengthening them lies not in abstract motivation, but in the design of our daily environments, choices, and tasks to include controlled doses of constructive difficulty.

One of the first domains where this must happen is in how we engage with information. The current norm is reactive consumption—notifications push content, feeds self-refresh, and headlines substitute for substance. Rebuilding cognitive stamina means reintroducing depth and slowness: *reading entire articles instead of summaries, exploring full texts over excerpts, delaying response to stimulus to process, contextualise, and reason.* This is not about ascetic withdrawal from modern tools, but about choosing formats and workflows that *demand more from the mind than passive scanning*. Information has to be earned, not merely received, to be retained in a way that builds endurance.

Consider also the structure of work. Much of knowledge work is now fragmented—tasks are slotted between calls, emails answered in bursts, attention toggled across multiple threads. These patterns optimise for responsiveness, not stamina. To rebuild that stamina, we need to *carve out zones of uninterrupted focus,* measured not just in time but in the depth of engagement achieved. A well-designed two-hour block of mentally demanding work builds far more stamina than a ten-hour day scattered with low-effort microtasks. It is this principle—*quality of exertion over volume of busyness*—

that defines cognitive conditioning. The goal is not to work more, but to work deeper.

A key component of this practice is what might be called voluntary difficulty: the conscious decision to choose the harder cognitive path when an easier one is available. This might mean solving a problem by hand before using a calculator, drafting arguments from first principles instead of relying on templates, or writing without grammar correction to force precision of thought. These are not nostalgic acts of technophobia, but *small disciplines of difficulty that compel the mind to stay in tension a little longer—where learning, creativity, and stamina are forged*. The point is not to be inefficient for its own sake, but to *intentionally resist the tendency toward automaticity and frictionlessness* that trains the brain to give up too soon.

Restoring challenge also means re-evaluating how we define 'progress'. Much of contemporary performance culture is calibrated for throughput and surface-level productivity: how fast, how many, how visible. But stamina-building work is rarely fast, often nonlinear, and usually invisible in its early stages. A researcher poring over raw data, a writer wrestling with a half-formed argument, a coder debugging a subtle error—these forms of thinking are rich in effort but poor in outward metrics. They don't translate easily into dashboards or KPIs, but *they are precisely the domains where cognitive stamina is stretched and strengthened.* Valuing this kind of work—slow, solitary, uncertain—requires both institutional and cultural recalibration.

Educational systems must play a central role in this restoration. If cognitive stamina is a muscle, then *school should be a gym,* not a performance stage. That means curricula that resist over-scaffolding, assessments that reward problem-framing over answer-matching, and learning environments that normalise frustration as part of the intellectual process. The temptation to 'engage' students through gamification or instant feedback should be balanced with the equally vital need to *toughen attention spans, deepen critical thinking, and build tolerance for delayed gratification.* What's required is not harsher discipline, but *better design of cognitive difficulty*: tasks that are not just challenging but *meaningfully so—designed to grow capacity rather than repel effort.*

Technology can be reimagined toward this end. Instead of being frictionless by default, tools can be built to *invite reflective pause, structured effort, and deeper interaction.* Writing apps that reward long-form drafting instead of stream-of-consciousness typing. Browsers that limit tab sprawl and prompt intentional search queries. Learning platforms that lock progression until concepts are demonstrably understood, not just clicked through. None of these innovations require abandoning tech; they require *reconfiguring it to partner with our cognitive development, not bypass it.* The goal is not to impose artificial hardship, but to restore necessary challenge.

There is also a psychological dimension to cognitive stamina: our relationship to boredom, delay, and uncertainty. The modern mind, conditioned by dopamine-rich stimuli, often interprets these states as intolerable rather than instructive. But from a developmental perspective, *boredom is not a failure of stimulation—it's a signal that the brain is ready to stretch beyond passive consumption.* Similarly, uncertainty is not paralysis but possibility—the tension that fuels hypothesis, exploration, and creativity. To rebuild stamina, we must learn to *stay present in these uncomfortable states,* not flee from them. And that begins with *daily practice*: meditating without entertainment, thinking before Googling, allowing conversations to unfold without interruption. These are small but radical acts of mental reconditioning.

Finally, none of this effort will take hold unless it is embedded in values. Rebuilding stamina requires a *shift in what we admire, pursue, and reward.* Depth over speed. Concentration over convenience. Complexity over simplification. These values must be modelled—by leaders who protect deep work time, educators who celebrate slow mastery, peers who challenge each other to think harder, not just faster. Culture, after all, is the long shadow of collective attention. And if that attention is shallow, impatient, and outsourced, stamina will vanish quietly within a single generation.

But the opposite is also true: if effort is re-integrated into how we live—deliberately, intelligently, consistently—the mind can regain its resilience. The human brain remains remarkably plastic, capable of profound re-adaptation at any age. It only asks for one thing: to be used fully, not just efficiently. To struggle meaningfully, not just operate smoothly. To think deeply, not just perform the appearance of thought. The path to that restoration is not mysterious. It begins with *choosing friction when ease is available, and returning to difficulty not with dread, but with purpose.* Because it is in difficulty—not ease—that the stamina to thrive, understand, and adapt is rebuilt.

Chapter 8
Cultural Amnesia

A civilisation does not vanish in a single cataclysm; it fades in convenience. What slips away first is rarely the monuments or objects themselves, but the memory of their connections—how past actions inform present choices, how enduring values guide behaviour, how wisdom is less a matter of knowing than of remembering. In an era awash with data, this may appear paradoxical. Yet to be surrounded by information is not the same as being grounded in memory. The contemporary mind is hyper-informed yet historically untethered: quick to retrieve, slow to recall; ever connected, yet rarely rooted.

This is not merely a cultural lapse. It is a consequence of systems designed to privilege immediacy. Digital platforms, real-time feeds, algorithmic prioritisation—all reward the ephemeral: trending over enduring, engagement over reflection, novelty over continuity. Culture now moves at a pace faster than it can be digested. Content scrolls past before it can be contextualised. News is consumed as spectacle, not processed as history. The self is re-authored daily, each iteration framed as a fresh performance rather than a cumulative narrative. Presentism—the inflation of the immediate at the expense of all else—is no longer a cognitive bias to correct; it is the default setting.

The consequences are profound. When memory is devalued, so too is meaning. Pattern recognition collapses. Intergenerational insight fractures. Decision-making flattens into reaction. Without memory, we misread context, unable to distinguish what is truly novel from what has merely been forgotten. Cultural amnesia is not simply a loss of knowledge; it is a weakening of the mind's defences against manipulation, repetition, and error. Without the ability to anchor ourselves in time, we become hyper-responsive to every fleeting signal, losing the pause required to ask: Have we seen this before? What lessons did we draw last time?

This erosion is deliberate in design. Many attention-shaping platforms treat forgetfulness as a feature rather than a flaw. Memory slows consumption; it encourages comparison, critical distance, and cumulative thinking—all threats to the frictionless novelty on which digital economies thrive. Stories vanish after twenty-four hours. Interfaces suppress the past. Search privileges recency over relevance. Even vast digital archives—emails, messages, photos—are so disorganised that recollection is deferred to algorithms or abandoned entirely. The result is structural: we become temporal amnesiacs, scrolling forward while thinking less.

Yet memory is not nostalgia. It is the architecture of continuity. In science, memory enables replication and refinement; in politics, it guards against the repetition of old errors; in personal development, it allows growth to be understood as a dialogue between who we were and who we are becoming. Memory underpins pattern recognition—the capacity to spot recurrence, contextualise change, and understand complexity across time. Without it, complexity becomes chaos, and novelty is indistinguishable from wisdom.

Tradition is often mistaken for dogma when, in truth, it represents accumulated pattern recognition across generations. To be traditional in its healthiest sense is not to obey blindly, but to carry forward insight while discarding error. Ritual, apprenticeship, oral storytelling, even cooking with elders—all functioned as distributed memory systems. Knowledge was not merely stored; it was enacted, refined through practice, embedded in community, and preserved in human muscle and custom rather than data alone.

Such embodied memory struggles to survive in the contemporary milieu. Learning is increasingly flattened into content. Videos are watched once and forgotten; ideas are skimmed but not integrated. Practice is replaced by exposure, and exposure is mistaken for understanding. The self becomes a curator of fragments, not a continuity of thought. There is always more to scroll into view, yet little time to metabolise what came before. It is intellectual consumption without digestion: abundance masking malnutrition.

Still, this loss is not irreversible. Memory can be cultivated, designed for, even wielded as a subtle form of resistance. To remember deliberately in a culture of instant forgetting is not to be backward-looking; it is to be intentional. It is a refusal to outsource meaning to algorithms, a refusal to treat history as optional context, a refusal to assume that only the immediate matters. Memory, in this sense, is autonomy: a reclamation of time, continuity, and discernment amid the churn of distraction.

Practices that restore anchored cognition abound. Long-form reading. Slow, reflective journaling. Revisiting old notebooks. Memorising poetry. Studying history as interconnected systems, not isolated events. Seeking guidance from elders. Returning to formative texts for renewed understanding. These are not quaint rituals but strategies for mental durability—ways to reconnect the present to the past, enabling decisions that are rooted rather than reactive. In a world of fleeting attention, such practices preserve sovereignty of mind.

The stakes are societal as well as personal. Societies that forget their trajectory become incoherent and ungovernable. Cultural memory underpins trust, accountability, and progress. Without it, we overreact to shocks, overcorrect at failures, and mistake repetition for innovation. Democracies falter not solely through attacks on truth, but when collective memory is too weak to defend it. Resilient culture demands narrative cohesion, and cohesion depends on memory. Knowing where we are is insufficient; we must remember how we arrived.

This chapter treats memory not as sentiment, but as an intellectual technology for complexity and wisdom. It examines how presentism distorts perspective, how design erodes recall, how tradition encodes learning, and how deliberate remembrance can restore both personal clarity and cultural coherence. The goal is not to abandon the present, but to reintegrate it into the broader story of who we are. In doing so, we remember not merely facts, but frameworks; not just events, but significance; not merely information, but identity.

The Rise of Presentism

A civilisation that forgets is not necessarily one that lacks access to information; it is often one that has grown addicted to immediacy. *Presentism*—the tendency to privilege the current moment over any other temporal dimension—has shifted from a cognitive bias into a full-blown cultural operating system. This is not simply a philosophical drift or a historical footnote. It is an engineered, systemic tilt in the architecture of our tools, our media, and increasingly, our minds. The internet was once heralded as a memory machine. Today, it functions more like a forgetting engine—streaming, refreshing, pushing forward without pause. What was said yesterday becomes irrelevant not because it was disproven, but because something newer has displaced it. *In a digital culture driven by the now, historical context is not refuted—it is rendered obsolete by velocity alone.*

This is not a neutral development. Presentism deforms attention, collapses perspective, and sabotages long-term thinking. It cultivates a worldview in which every issue appears unprecedented, every crisis novel, and every opinion free-floating from precedent. When yesterday's insight is displaced by today's feed, we no longer argue over history—we simply forget it. Worse, we begin to mistake forgetting for progress. Real-time culture becomes not just a tempo but a worldview. It trains us to value what is current over what is consequential, what is trending over what is true.

The psychological impact is as profound as the cultural one. Continuous immersion in the now fosters a kind of cognitive flattening: our mental maps become short-range, our judgments shallow, our moral reasoning impulsive. We react rather than reflect. Without access to a longer frame of

reference, we lose the ability to compare, to contextualise, to trace the trajectory of events. The present dominates not because it is more accurate but because it is more accessible—and because the architecture of our attention has been recalibrated to reward immediacy over insight. *The algorithm does not ask what you need to remember—it serves what you cannot resist clicking.*

This recalibration is not accidental. Real-time culture is profitable. Attention platforms—from social media giants to news aggregators—are financially incentivised to keep users in a state of perpetual scroll. Novelty drives engagement, and engagement drives data, which in turn fuels the predictive algorithms that monetise behavioural forecasting. But the cost of this convenience is cumulative: we forget more than we realise, and we realise it less and less. *The present becomes a feedback loop, amplifying the familiar, echoing the urgent, and eroding the unfamiliar terrain of the past.*

It would be one thing if this transformation affected only media consumption. But it now bleeds into institutions once tasked with preserving historical memory. Education bends towards testable outcomes rather than intellectual continuity. Politics becomes reactive rather than deliberative. Public discourse accelerates until there is no time for synthesis. Newsrooms cover stories for clicks, not context. Even scientific inquiry faces pressure to produce immediate results at the expense of longitudinal rigour. *The institutions built to steward memory are increasingly shaped by the tempo of platforms designed to erase it.*

Yet the loss of long-term memory is not merely academic. It has practical consequences at every level of decision-making. Take environmental policy: a short-term mindset struggles to reckon with climate processes that unfold across decades. In medicine, breakthroughs that took years of cumulative effort are now marketed as momentary 'disruptions,' with little attention to lineage. In social justice, movements risk detaching from the very histories that give their claims depth and moral force. *To confront the present wisely requires remembering the past with fidelity.*

This phenomenon is further complicated by the rise of revisionist memory—where selective fragments of history are resurfaced algorithmically, shorn of context and deployed to reinforce contemporary bias. A historical quote gains traction not because it is representative, but because it is shareable. A statistic is circulated not because it is accurate, but because it aligns with tribal narratives. *Presentism, in this sense, is not just forgetfulness—it is the hyper-curation of memory to suit the momentary mood of the crowd.* Context collapses, and complexity becomes a liability. The past is not merely forgotten; it is weaponised in fragments.

Contrast this with the function of memory in traditional societies. Oral traditions, religious texts, apprenticeship models, and intergenerational storytelling were not nostalgic mechanisms—they were adaptive ones. They encoded trial-and-error knowledge, behavioural norms, and value systems that enabled group survival over time. Memory served as an epistemological anchor: a way to discern not only what had been done before, but what patterns were likely to repeat. In many Indigenous cultures, elders are not viewed as repositories of static wisdom, but as dynamic interpreters of long-form memory—able to advise not because they predict the future, but because they remember the past deeply enough to spot echoes in the present. *This is not history as trivia. It is memory as strategy.*

By contrast, modern digital memory is both shallow and fragmented. We outsource recollection to search engines, calendars, and cloud services, rarely revisiting our own internal archives. Autocomplete completes our thoughts. Memories are stored but not rehearsed. *We accumulate data without metabolising experience.* This shift erodes not only our capacity for retention, but our very intuition of time. Linear sequence breaks down; cause and effect blur. The mind becomes reactive, always poised for the next ping but rarely rooted in any coherent before.

Ironically, our devices are more memory-capable than ever. We photograph everything, record meetings, archive every message—but rarely return to any of it. The very act of documenting becomes a substitute for remembering. Why reflect, when you can replay? Why internalise, when you can retrieve? But *retrieval is not recollection.* To remember something is to weave it into the evolving structure of the self. It is to make meaning from experience. Data storage alone does not achieve this. Reflection, integration, and pattern recognition do.

So what is lost when presentism becomes the dominant mode of consciousness? Most fundamentally, we lose *narrative coherence*. The ability to make sense of ourselves as situated beings—in families, in histories, in civilisations—is undermined. We mistake our timelines for identity, our notifications for relevance, our moments of visibility for progress. The self becomes a bundle of reactions instead of a continuous becoming. *Without the thread of memory, we drift into solipsism: each day becomes its own world, disconnected from the one before.*

But memory can be rehabilitated—not simply as storage, but as *a cognitive and cultural discipline*. To resist presentism is not to retreat into nostalgia, but to reclaim perspective. It involves choosing slow media over fast feeds. Returning to long-form reading. Practising reflection as a daily habit. Studying history not as a moral fable, but as a rigorous inquiry into cause, consequence, and continuity. It means building personal and institutional rhythms that support recollection, not just reaction. *It means designing for time, not just for speed.*

Crucially, this shift also calls for philosophical clarity. Presentism is not just a technical issue—it is an ethical one. It asks whether we believe wisdom is cumulative or momentary. Whether we see ourselves as isolated agents or as stewards of inherited knowledge. Whether we act for attention or for legacy. These are not abstract questions. They play out every day in the design of technology, the structure of institutions, and the habits of individual attention.

To resist presentism is to honour continuity over content, depth over reaction, memory over momentum. It is to reassert the mind's ability to contextualise, to synthesise, and to resist the coercion of the now. In doing so, we do not abandon the present—we reclaim it as part of a larger story.

Forgetfulness as a Design Feature

A system that forgets is not necessarily broken—it may be functioning exactly as intended. In today's digital economy, forgetfulness is not an accident of scale or oversight, but a commercially advantageous feature embedded into the architecture of our most frequented platforms. The compulsive refresh of newsfeeds, the vanishing nature of stories, the burial of old conversations beneath endless scroll—all reflect an implicit design preference: value the new, discard the old. What might look like rapid obsolescence of content is often, in fact, a deliberately constructed amnesia engine. This isn't a side-effect of digital modernity; it's the business model.

Tech platforms thrive on novelty. Not just new features, but new content, new trends, new emotions. The acceleration of the content cycle creates the illusion of relevance while dulling the capacity to recall, reflect, or critically integrate what came before. The user's attention is funnelled into the ever-unfolding present, where context is expendable and retention is neither encouraged nor rewarded. This creates a strategic convenience for the platform: a user whose memory is shortened is a user who re-engages more often, who scrolls more, who forgets what they've already seen and is therefore more susceptible to seeing it again—repackaged, reframed, resurfaced as 'fresh.'

This ephemeral design logic is not confined to social media. Recommendation algorithms on platforms like Netflix, Spotify, or YouTube rarely prompt users to revisit previously watched or listened content. Instead, they serve up the next thing—tailored for immediate appeal, frictionless consumption, and minimal contemplation. The systems are optimised not for enrichment, understanding, or depth of knowledge, but for sustained engagement, which is to say, sustained monetisation. What you consumed yesterday is functionally erased in favour of what you are nudged to consume next. Your digital past—preferences, clicks, views—is not preserved for your benefit, but rather mined and abstracted to manipulate your future behaviour.

In this framework, memory becomes commercially inconvenient. A user who remembers may also become more discerning. They may resist manipulation, question the repetition of ideas, or notice the recycling of sentiment. Worse still, they might grow bored or restless—not because the world is dull, but because the digital world is repeating itself under the guise of infinite novelty. The erosion of historical context in digital space is thus not merely a cultural shift; it is a calculated degradation that benefits those who profit from distraction, churn, and consumer volatility.

Even more telling is how this forgetfulness reshapes personal identity. When our digital histories are made inaccessible—or buried under noise—we begin to internalise that amnesia. We forget past curiosities, evolving opinions, previous emotional states. Our digital selves become a perpetual now, a flat continuity of preference with no visible arc of change. Growth is rendered illegible. Contrast this with a bookshelf, a photo album, or even a personal journal—objects that invite reflection and reconstruction of memory. These analog artefacts are memory scaffolds. Their digital counterparts are sandcastles washed away with each algorithmic tide.

Consider how this dynamic affects civic and collective memory. When yesterday's outrage is algorithmically overwritten by today's trend, political attention fragments. Movements lose momentum. Structural critique dissolves into ambient grumbling. Social media platforms claim neutrality in this process, yet the design of attention hierarchies makes them active participants in what is remembered and what is discarded. When virality becomes the arbiter of visibility, endurance is eclipsed by immediacy. Causes must continually rebrand themselves to stay afloat in an ecosystem that forgets by design.

There is also a deeper cognitive toll. When digital environments constantly displace the old with the new, we lose not only memory but the *habit* of memory. Mental architectures that rely on revisiting, revising, and recontextualising begin to atrophy. Reflection becomes foreign. Pattern recognition dulls. Learning fragments into disconnected insights, with no thread to bind them into a coherent worldview. In effect, we become informationally overweight and interpretively undernourished.

To resist this drift toward digital forgetting requires effort—and more importantly, intention. It means deliberately retaining what platforms seek to erase. It may involve maintaining personal archives, using tools that prioritise retrieval over novelty, or slowing down consumption to allow for integration. It means reintroducing cognitive friction into systems designed for ease. And at the cultural level, it demands that we examine not just what we remember, but who decides what is worth remembering.

The economic incentives that drive platform forgetfulness are unlikely to shift voluntarily. The burden of memory, therefore, falls on individuals, institutions, and subcultures that choose to value it. Whether in education, media, or personal practice, the act of remembering must be treated as a deliberate stance—one that counters the commercial logic of erasure. Otherwise, we risk becoming not only forgetful, but unremembering—unable to hold continuity of thought, feeling, or identity in a world perpetually updated to obscure its own past.

Tradition, Practice, and Pattern Recognition

In a world saturated with information, the rarest asset is not data, but discernment. It is no longer difficult to acquire facts—what's difficult is knowing which ones matter, how they fit together, and what they imply. This is the domain not of information but of wisdom. And wisdom, unlike knowledge, is not downloaded or indexed—it is grown through the soil of memory, watered by repetition, and matured through reflection. What we often call "intuition" in accomplished thinkers or seasoned professionals is usually the visible tip of a submerged structure: a deep memory lattice built over years of exposure, pattern recognition, and distilled learning. Strip that away and what remains is cognitive shallowness masquerading as flexibility.

The undervaluing of memory in modern digital culture has created a paradoxical illusion. We appear to know more, because we have access to more. But *having access* is not the same as *having integration*. A search engine can retrieve; it cannot understand. An archive can store; it cannot synthesise. Without memory—the long-term, often effortful, process of internalising, comparing, and embedding knowledge across time—there is no platform for wisdom to stand on. *Memory is not an inert warehouse; it is an active organ of insight.* It allows us to trace trajectories, recognise false patterns, avoid naive repetitions, and see through short-term noise to long-term significance.

Tradition, in this context, is memory externalised across generations. It encodes collective learnings—cultural, ethical, artistic, epistemological—that individuals could not live long enough to acquire firsthand. Its utility is not that it is always right, but that it prevents each generation from starting again with blank cognitive slate. Dismissing tradition as outdated is often a failure to understand what it conserves: not rigidity, but relevance distilled through time. When traditions are lost without examination, what disappears is not just form, but the *memory of function*. We forget why certain practices evolved, what problems they once solved, what dilemmas they refined.

This forgetting is not neutral—it has consequences. For instance, in professional domains like medicine, law, or architecture, the mastery of underlying principles depends on more than procedural compliance. A seasoned clinician does not simply follow diagnostic checklists; they recognise patterns that are not yet explicit. They draw on cases remembered, on contradictions observed, on tacit knowledge accumulated through practice. Their competence is not merely computational—it is heuristic, experiential, narrative. In such domains, *the erosion of memory is the erosion of depth*. Professionals become technicians. Problem-solvers become proceduralists.

The same pattern holds in cultural life. When oral storytelling gave way to digital feeds, the rhythm of narrative was not the only thing lost. Also lost was the social function of retelling, the cumulative wisdom embedded in repetition, and the subtle calibration of memory to meaning. Rituals, whether religious or secular, were never just about belief. They were practices of attention, repositories of memory, methods of aligning individual experience with larger, inherited frames. Their disappearance leaves behind an unanchored present: hyperconnected yet ahistorical, expressive yet unmoored.

To understand the role of memory in wisdom is to understand the role of *pattern recognition*. Insight does not emerge from isolated novelty; it emerges when the new collides with the remembered. A child encountering fire for the first time may be fascinated, but a scientist encountering a new form of combustion compares it to every flame they've known. In this comparison, pattern recognition functions not as a shortcut but as an *engine of meaning*. Every insight rests on the tension between old and new. It is only through accumulated memory that this contrast becomes visible.

Modern machine learning offers a curious parallel. Algorithms trained on massive datasets begin to detect subtle correlations and hidden regularities—so long as the data is coherent and rich. But imagine feeding such systems only recent, scattered, or contradictory data. The models become erratic, brittle, biased. Human cognition is no different. *When memory is thin, pattern recognition becomes distorted.* We become vulnerable to misfiring analogies, premature conclusions, and shallow correlations. This is why practice—deliberate, repeated exposure to meaningful variation—is indispensable. It is through practice that memory is not only formed, but made resilient.

Importantly, practice is not just about doing; it is about remembering what one has done, refining it, and comparing it with prior effort. In music, for instance, playing a scale without memory is mechanical. Playing it with memory means noting tone, fluidity, error patterns—mentally tracking improvement. The same holds in writing, coding, athletics, or philosophy. *Practice without memory is labour; practice with memory is learning.* The presence of memory is what allows feedback to matter. Without it, each repetition is isolated, incapable of accumulating into skill.

There is a moral dimension to this as well. In civic life, memory undergirds the capacity for justice. Societies that forget their histories—of violence, of exclusion, of triumph and failure—are societies that cannot reason morally about the present. Historical amnesia does not make us freer; it makes us manipulable. It severs causality. It allows patterns of harm to re-emerge under new names. Thus, the preservation of memory through education, commemoration, and collective practice is not sentimentalism—it is civilisational maintenance.

Yet we increasingly design tools that displace memory. Auto-suggestions complete our thoughts. Notifications override recall. Cloud storage outsources retention. Recommendation engines flatten preference into popularity. In the name of ease, we have decoupled remembering from using. *This is not merely a convenience; it is a de-skilling.* The more we outsource memory, the more we reduce our capacity to discriminate, to relate, to infer. What begins as time-saving becomes mind-thinning.

To reverse this trend, memory must be treated as a faculty worth training, not merely as a repository to digitise. This does not mean rejecting technology, but recalibrating its relationship to cognition. Tools should support pattern recognition, not short-circuit it. They should enable reflection, not perpetuate acceleration. At the individual level, cultivating memory might involve intentional re-reading, manual note-taking, story retelling, or ritualised reflection. At the institutional level, it might mean embedding traditions of review, narrative, or mentorship into education and governance.

Ultimately, wisdom is not a spark of genius, but a pattern built over time—through memory, through practice, through disciplined attention to the shapes that knowledge forms across experience. In a culture intoxicated by immediacy, the most radical act may simply be to remember—and in remembering, to see.

Memory as Resistance

The most subversive thing a person can do in a forgetful culture is to remember. Not simply to recall information, but to remember with depth, deliberation, and defiance. This kind of remembering is not nostalgic—it is strategic. It reclaims continuity where others impose rupture. It refuses to let the past be overwritten by the next notification. *In an environment designed to erase context and flatten time, memory becomes a form of cultural and cognitive autonomy.*

When the daily feed insists that only the present matters—that only today's outrage, trend, or disaster is real—then remembering becomes political. To remember deeply is to resist the compulsion to be constantly reactive. It is to retain frames of reference that expose repetition, illusion, and manipulation. Memory gives us distance, and with distance comes discernment. It becomes possible to ask: Have we seen this before? What was the outcome? What was learned—and what was ignored?

This mode of remembering stands apart from archival accumulation. Data storage is not memory. Your browser history, cloud drives, and app analytics retain more than you ever could, but they do not remember in any meaningful sense. *To remember is not to access; it is to integrate.* It requires reflection, contextualisation, emotional processing, and moral anchoring. It cannot be outsourced. Nor can it be fully automated—because memory, when it truly functions, is inseparable from agency.

Technological systems increasingly rely on selective forgetfulness—not as a bug, but as a design feature. Social media timelines bury past posts beneath a river of novelty. Streaming platforms prioritise trending content over curated archives. News apps cycle headlines every few hours, regardless of continuity. *These architectures do not just fail to preserve memory—they actively discourage it.* The user is not supposed to look back. Retention becomes friction. Reflection becomes a lag in the dopamine loop.

This systemic presentism is not neutral. It serves specific interests. In advertising, forgetting the past ensures a consumer remains perpetually impressionable—more likely to follow the latest impulse than to compare it with previous purchases or previous promises. In politics, a public with poor memory cannot hold leaders accountable; it lacks the narrative thread to track hypocrisy or see long-term consequences. In social movements, historical forgetting weakens the moral force of precedents—it isolates each struggle from the lineage of those that came before.

The psychological consequences are equally significant. Without a robust memory, identity becomes fragmented. Who one is becomes indistinguishable from what one reacts to. Decision-making, stripped of temporal depth, becomes impulsive rather than principled. The ability to endure complexity, to sit with ambiguity, or to tolerate delay—all of which depend on sustained memory—erodes under the weight of real-time culture. *This is not only a loss of cognitive integrity; it is a loss of selfhood.*

Yet this is precisely why remembering deliberately is a radical act. It restores personal and collective continuity. It reconnects past experience to present judgment. It allows individuals to form convictions that are not simply reactions, but conclusions—reached, revised, and reinforced over time. To remember is to reclaim narrative authorship. It is to resist the condition of being perpetually reset by the next prompt, headline, or trend.

Memory as resistance also reveals itself in cultural practice. When indigenous communities document oral histories, when diasporas preserve ancestral languages, when descendants honour rituals banned or erased by colonisers, they are not preserving the past for its own sake. They are *asserting the right to define reality on their own terms*. Memory, in such cases, is a form of survival—not of bodies, but of epistemologies. What is remembered determines what is possible. And what is forgotten is often what those in power would prefer to remain unexamined.

Educational institutions, long seen as memory-keepers of civilisations, are themselves increasingly drawn into the gravitational pull of digital immediacy. Curricula are streamlined. History is reframed to fit political convenience. Students are encouraged to "move fast" and "think forward"—as if the past had nothing essential to teach, except as trivia or warning. *But speed without memory is not innovation—it is drift.* Genuine learning requires the anchoring of memory: the ability to connect texts, theories, events, and consequences across time.

This is why intellectual maturity depends not just on learning new things, but on retaining—and re-evaluating—what one has already learned. A thinker without memory is merely a stimulus processor, not a synthesiser. And a society that loses its memory may remain technologically advanced, but it will become epistemologically brittle. It will rediscover the same problems repeatedly, and mistake recurrence for novelty.

Even on the individual level, to remember—when done with intention—can be an act of healing. Trauma research shows that unprocessed experiences often return in intrusive, fragmentary forms. Recovery, paradoxically, involves remembering—not to re-injure, but to integrate. To name, contextualise, and contain. This psychological process mirrors the cultural imperative: *remembering enables wholeness*. Without it, both minds and societies fracture under the burden of unassimilated experience.

Of course, not all memory is redemptive. There are distortions, fixations, and dogmas masquerading as memory. But the antidote to bad memory is not amnesia—it is deeper memory. More honest, more critical, more complete. Memory as resistance is not the clinging to myth, but the refusal to let meaning be flattened. It is the willingness to carry forward what is unresolved, so that it might yet inform what is becoming.

In practical terms, cultivating memory as resistance may involve small, deliberate acts. Keeping a handwritten journal, revisiting books rather than only consuming new ones, studying history not as a list of dates but as a pattern of ideas and structures. It may mean resisting algorithmic feeds in favour of curated archives, or making space for long-form media in place of scrollable fragments. *These choices may seem minor, but over time they reshape what the mind holds onto—and what it lets go.*

They also restore sovereignty. A person who remembers well—who builds continuity between thoughts, experiences, and convictions—is harder to persuade, harder to distract, and harder to deceive. They become less susceptible to the tyranny of the now. They see that many things which present themselves as urgent are in fact recycled. Many that appear new are echoes. And many that seem harmless are corrosive only when forgotten.

Memory is not resistance because it is nostalgic. It is resistance because it is anchoring. It creates depth in a culture that rewards surface. It protects discernment in a climate that rewards noise. And it enables freedom of thought in systems that prefer reaction to reflection. *To remember is to remain intact when the culture around you becomes a blur.* It is to insist on time's fullness when everything else insists on the moment.

There is no app for this. No shortcut, no patch. Only the slow, difficult, sovereign work of carrying forward what matters—and refusing to forget what should never have been erased.

Chapter 9
Designing for Dependency

Step into any room with Wi-Fi, and the scene is almost ritualistic: heads bent, eyes locked, fingers flicking across screens. What seems like casual interaction with technology is, on closer inspection, a subtler choreography—one that nudges behaviour toward dependence. Tools we describe as "user-friendly" are, in many respects, user-dependent by design. Convenience masks a cultivated inertia. We are not merely using our devices; we are shaped by them—drawn toward passivity, nudged toward compulsiveness, and distanced from independence.

This dependency is no accident. It flows from a design logic centred on what the tech industry calls "stickiness." A sticky product is not just used; it is returned to reflexively. More time-on-platform generates monetisable data, more advertising impressions, higher valuations. Attention is not incidental; it is the business model. Consequently, the user experience is sculpted with a singular aim: prevent disengagement.

From infinite scrolls to notification badges, from autoplay to algorithmically curated feeds, each interaction is layered with reinforcement. Platforms borrow variable reward schedules from gambling psychology, encouraging intermittent gratification. Cognitive load is reduced—not to ease stress, but to remove friction that might prompt exit. Push alerts intrude not for urgency, but to maintain proximity. The tool ceases to be optional; it becomes ambient, omnipresent.

Yet there is a deeper cost. Such design fosters learned helplessness. When barriers are removed, decisions automated, and needs anticipated, users relinquish more than effort—they lose orientation. Navigation turns into selection, curiosity into passive consumption, initiative into nudged compliance. The more "intuitive" the interface, the less we perceive what it displaces: memory, patience, deliberation, restraint.

Ease is seductive, and there is logic to it: make things simple, and more people will engage. But ease is never neutral. It reconfigures the relationship between person and task, intention and action, idea and effort. A calculator simplifies arithmetic, but does not eliminate understanding; GPS aids navigation, yet dulls the mental maps once internalised. Pursuing frictionless design risks infantilising the user. Empowerment, in this context, often slides into enfeeblement—an interface so seamless that participation itself vanishes.

The ethical implications are significant, though frequently overlooked. UX patterns optimised for engagement without accountability become behavioural traps. Platforms purport to serve users, but more often serve monetisation incentives. When the path of least resistance is the only path presented, choice collapses into compliance. There is a subtle tyranny in comfort—a quiet erosion of autonomy and dignity.

This dependency is reinforced by the political economy of attention. In a digital marketplace, every click is a commodity, every scroll a transaction. The mind is not the customer; it is the product. Cognitive offloading—allowing algorithms to pick songs, routes, posts, purchases—renders the user predictable and, therefore, more valuable. Less deviation equals higher commodification.

The same logic extends beyond consumer apps. Enterprise software, productivity platforms, educational tools increasingly adopt stickiness principles: streamlined workflows, nudged behaviours, gamified compliance. What erodes in this process is judgment. When systems anticipate each next move, decisions are no longer self-directed. The user becomes conditioned, a participant in a loop designed by another.

Still, countercurrents exist. A growing cohort of designers and thinkers challenge the moral foundations of behavioural design. Human-centred design was intended to amplify capability, not suppress it. The question shifts from how to make systems easier to how to make them honourable: design for dignity, not addiction; for agency, not automation. This may involve reintroducing friction—purposefully.

Consider a text editor without autocorrect, compelling the user to confront spelling errors. A focus app that delays notifications rather than interrupting. A recommendation engine that suggests not only what is familiar, but what challenges and expands thinking. These are not technological impossibilities—they are philosophical choices. Design can erode effort or cultivate it; the difference is intention.

Reconceptualising usability means asking new questions: what kind of effort is meaningful? Where should stopping points allow reflection? How can time be designed well, rather than merely filled? It requires rejecting the default assumption that users exist primarily as engagement nodes, and returning to the notion of the user as thinker, learner, maker—not simply responder. This is not nostalgia; it is a quiet radicalism, reasserting design's original aspiration: to amplify human potential.

In the following chapters, we will examine the mechanics of dependency, interrogate its ethical scaffolding, and explore how design might be redirected toward generative, human-respecting systems—ones that treat users not as captives, but as minds worthy of cultivation. Because the way we design our systems ultimately shapes not only how users act, but how we, collectively, define ourselves.

The Logic of Stickiness

When a user opens a social media app for a momentary distraction and resurfaces forty-five minutes later, unsure of where the time went, this is not incidental. It is the intended outcome of a product design logic honed to precision. Behind the sleek interfaces of consumer technology lies a less visible architecture of influence—one engineered not to assist, but to *absorb*. The dominant metric of success for most digital platforms is not usefulness, but *retention*. In the parlance of product managers and behavioural scientists, the goal is "stickiness": how effectively a platform keeps a user engaged, how often they return, how difficult it becomes to disengage. This logic has become the central nervous system of our digital lives, quietly remapping the contours of attention, autonomy, and cognition.

Stickiness is a deceptively benign term. It evokes convenience, familiarity, perhaps even utility. But in practice, it represents a constellation of tactics—some psychological, some aesthetic, others algorithmic—geared towards fostering dependency. Platforms like Instagram, YouTube, TikTok, and Netflix don't merely deliver content; they deliver it in a sequence and form calculated to minimise cognitive interruption and maximise behavioural continuation. The infinite scroll was not an innovation in usability, but in *captivity*. When the end of content is always just a swipe away, disengagement becomes effortful. The platform does not require commitment—it demands *inertia*.

The commercial rationale is straightforward. The more time a user spends on a platform, the more advertising inventory can be sold, the more behavioural data can be extracted, and the more tightly calibrated the experience can become. Stickiness is, fundamentally, *a business model built on behavioural predictability*. In this economy, friction is failure; interruption is leakage; reflection is risk. The ideal user is not the one who thinks critically or leaves satisfied, but the one who returns compulsively.

These principles are not merely abstract. Consider the specific case of TikTok's content feed. Unlike traditional social networks where a user selects content from people they follow, TikTok's "For You" page begins curating instantly. The algorithm learns from every scroll, every pause, every swipe away. Within minutes, the feed becomes finely attuned to the user's affective responses—curating not what they *ought* to see, but what they *can't* stop watching. This is not user preference, but behavioural entrainment. *The app learns you faster than you learn yourself.*

Such systems are often justified as adaptive and personalised. But what they adapt to is not aspiration—it is impulse. What they personalise is not growth—it is gratification. This is the core of the stickiness logic: *create an experience so frictionless, so neurologically rewarding, that the user loses all awareness of their own drift*. In traditional design, the goal was utility. In sticky design, the goal is habituation.

This shift is not ethically neutral. The more a system leans into stickiness, the more it erodes user independence. A platform that anticipates every desire before it is consciously formed begins to collapse the distinction between will and response. Autonomy becomes illusory. The user is no longer *choosing* to engage—they are *being managed* into engagement. This is not technological assistance, but behavioural orchestration.

Even the language of the industry betrays its intentions. Design elements are described as "retention hooks," "trigger loops," and "habit-forming cues." Techniques drawn from behavioural psychology—like the use of intermittent variable rewards—are deliberately deployed to foster compulsive patterns. These are the same psychological principles used in casino design: keep the user uncertain about their next reward, and they will keep playing. The user becomes a subject of operant conditioning, rewarded not for exploration or insight, but for attention alone.

Crucially, the logic of stickiness is not restricted to entertainment platforms. Productivity tools, fitness apps, even educational software now embed similar tactics. Duolingo, for instance, uses streaks and gamified milestones to foster daily returns. On the surface, this appears motivational. But over time, the cognitive framing shifts: learning becomes secondary to *preserving the streak*. The user is retained, but the substance of engagement is hollowed out.

This illustrates a larger problem. When platforms optimise for retention, *quality of engagement declines*. Time-on-task becomes more important than depth of thought. A video watched half-attentively still counts as a view. A quiz completed while distracted still counts as participation. The user is deemed "active," even as their mental agency is passive. The metric rewards presence, not presence of mind.

A subtler consequence is the gradual reshaping of user expectation. As sticky design becomes ubiquitous, *we come to expect engagement without effort*. Boredom becomes intolerable. Reflection becomes inconvenient. Any task requiring delayed gratification feels poorly designed. In such an environment, deep work—reading, writing, critical analysis—feels alien. Not because it is obsolete, but because the friction it entails is no longer normalised. The logic of stickiness has rewired what we find cognitively reasonable.

Some might argue that stickiness is simply good business. After all, if users keep returning, that must indicate value. But this is an illusion born of narrowed definition. Returning to a platform does not mean it served the user's best interest. It means the platform made leaving uncomfortable. *There is a difference between being useful and being difficult to quit.*

This tension is amplified in young users, whose cognitive habits are still forming. A child who grows up in sticky ecosystems does not merely consume content differently—they *think* differently. Expectation for instant feedback, difficulty with sustained attention, aversion to ambiguity—these are not personal failures, but systemically encouraged defaults. Platforms that prize stickiness *train the mind to anticipate stimulation rather than construct understanding*.

To understand this logic more fully, we must ask: what would *non-sticky* design look like? It would value disengagement as much as engagement. It would include intentional stopping points—end-of-feed prompts, natural session limits, content summaries. It would privilege clarity over compulsion. It would track meaningful metrics—comprehension, reflection, transformation—rather than mere time-spent. In short, it would honour the user's time and attention as finite, not exploitable.

Some designers and thinkers are beginning to resist the tyranny of stickiness. Tools like the Light Phone, which intentionally limit functionality, or software that encourages time-blocked usage, are early signs of a countercurrent. But these remain niche. The dominant ecosystem still favours models that conflate usability with dependency.

To break from this logic requires more than better features. It demands a shift in ethos: from retention to respect, from manipulation to trust. The challenge is not to make tools less effective, but to redefine what effectiveness means. *Is a platform successful because it keeps you there, or because it leaves you stronger when you go?*

This is not a Luddite appeal, nor a nostalgic yearning for pre-digital purity. It is a call for intellectual and ethical clarity. *Design is not just about what a product does; it is about what it demands in return.* And in the age of stickiness, the cost is not money—it is mental freedom. The logic of stickiness has already reshaped how we spend our time. The more urgent question is whether we want it to reshape *who we become*.

Behavioural Design and the Ethics of Ease

Ease is the modern gospel of user experience design. The ideal interface is said to be "intuitive," the preferred flow "frictionless," and the pinnacle of success "seamless." From streaming platforms to banking apps, from online shopping carts to meditation tools, the design mandate is clear: reduce cognitive load, remove decision points, and smooth the user's journey until no effort remains. But ease, for all its surface benevolence, is not ethically neutral. The assumption that easier is better rests on a moral shortfall—

the conflation of convenience with care, and automation with empowerment. Beneath the polished aesthetic of modern interfaces lies a deeper question: *what are we optimising for, and at what cost to the user's agency, understanding, and growth?*

Behavioural design, as a discipline, is the application of psychological insights into interface design to guide user actions. Rooted in cognitive science and behavioural economics, it emerged as a pragmatic way to help people make better choices. The early promise was noble: nudge users toward saving more, eating better, learning faster. In its more cautious applications, it remains a useful and humane approach to shaping behaviour for good. But over time, the field has drifted. The dominant use-case today is not behavioural support, but behavioural *extraction*. Instead of helping users do what they *want*, most systems now guide them to do what *platforms want*. And this distinction is not merely functional—it is moral.

Consider the typical food delivery app. Its design removes every friction point between appetite and action. Search bars autocomplete your cravings; favourites are pre-saved; tips are suggested; repeat orders are two taps away. In theory, this represents good service. In practice, it displaces intention with impulse. What was once a decision—what to eat, when to eat it, whether to cook—is now a reflex. *The architecture of ease transforms desire into default.*

Such experiences are sold to users under the banner of efficiency, but this framing ignores the ethical asymmetry of the transaction. When a user's effort is reduced, their awareness is reduced in parallel. And in this thinning of cognitive engagement lies the platform's power. It is far easier to upsell, distract, or redirect a user who is not paying attention. The smoother the journey, the less likely the traveller is to ask where they're going—or who's paying for the ride. *Ease creates passivity, and passivity invites manipulation.*

This is not a theoretical danger. Look to the design of subscription services. Free trials roll into paid accounts by default. Cancellation requires multiple steps, hidden menus, or oddly timed prompts. These so-called "dark patterns" are not bugs in behavioural design—they are its natural outcome when ease is decoupled from ethics. They capitalise on forgetfulness, inertia, and ambiguity. The system *appears* user-friendly, even as it takes advantage of the very behaviours it has conditioned.

The same dynamic plays out in learning platforms. Consider the rise of algorithmically curated educational content. Apps promise to "make learning easy" by delivering bite-sized facts, gamified quizzes, and minimal challenge. But education is not entertainment. *Real learning requires struggle, reflection, and synthesis—none of which are particularly easy.* When design prioritises retention metrics over cognitive development, the result is a superficial engagement that flatters but does not fortify the mind. Students feel productive while remaining fundamentally unchanged.

These trends reflect a broader epistemic shift: the idea that *good design means eliminating effort*. But effort, in many human contexts, is not a flaw to be engineered away—it is the crucible in which understanding forms. Engagement, after all, is not just interaction—it is investment. It is attention sharpened by challenge. When systems are designed to remove all resistance, they remove the very conditions under which users learn, grow, and decide for themselves.

And here lies the ethical fulcrum. Behavioural design does not merely shape action—it shapes *character*. If we are continually presented with interfaces that anticipate our needs, fill in our thoughts, and deliver outcomes without friction, we lose something essential: *the practice of navigating ambiguity, of making trade-offs, of confronting complexity*. These are not just skills; they are civic virtues. They prepare us not just to shop and scroll, but to vote, to reason, to care.

Of course, some ease is necessary. No one wishes for deliberately inefficient systems. But there is a moral distinction between *accessibility* and *infantilisation*. A design that enables the elderly to navigate government services with clarity is humane. A design that tricks them into accepting pre-selected options they don't understand is exploitative. The line between helping and handling the user is thin, and it demands constant ethical scrutiny.

Yet this scrutiny is often absent in commercial design culture. Product teams are rewarded for engagement metrics, not epistemic outcomes. Designers are taught to A/B test for click-through, not for comprehension. In such environments, ethical considerations become marginal—a checkbox at best, a marketing afterthought at worst. The system optimises what it can measure, and what it can measure is usually ease. Not reflection, not understanding, not flourishing.

This presents a philosophical tension. The very tools that allow us to reduce effort in design—behavioural insights, persuasive interface patterns, predictive analytics—are morally agnostic. They can be used to promote health or addiction, agency or automation. The question is not whether we *can* make something easy, but whether we *should*. And the answer must rest on a deeper understanding of what human beings require not just to function, but to *thrive*.

To move forward, behavioural design must abandon its infatuation with frictionless experiences and begin to embrace what might be called *constructive friction*. These are design elements that invite engagement rather than bypass it. A platform might, for instance, ask the user to reflect before making a decision, or delay gratification to promote better judgment. These are not obstacles—they are opportunities for *growth*. They recognise that *ease should be in service of the user's goals, not the platform's profits.*

In public policy, there are early signs of such ethical recalibration. Some governments have begun regulating manipulative interfaces under digital consumer protection frameworks. The EU's General Data Protection Regulation (GDPR) requires that consent be explicit and informed—an effort to dismantle the exploitative elegance of pre-ticked boxes and hidden defaults. These moves represent not just legal correction, but philosophical resistance: a reassertion of agency in the face of design that seeks to erode it.

But lasting change will require more than regulation. It demands a cultural shift within the design community itself. Designers must be trained not only in usability but in moral reasoning. They must be asked not just what will work, but *for whom, in what context,* and *with what long-term effect.* Universities, bootcamps, and corporate training programmes must teach that design is not just a tool—it is a form of governance. Every interface makes choices about what is visible, what is emphasised, and what is deferred. Those choices shape cognition, shape behaviour, and ultimately shape society.

To design ethically in an age of ease is to acknowledge that users are not merely consumers—they are citizens, learners, patients, parents, people. And people deserve more than smooth surfaces and frictionless flows. They deserve systems that *respect their intelligence, honour their complexity, and demand their attention where it matters most.* This is not a rejection of behavioural design. It is a call to elevate it—to return it to its highest purpose: *not to control the user, but to support their freedom.*

In a world awash with convenience, the true mark of ethical design may not be how much it removes—but how much it invites us to *re-engage with the effort of being human.*

The Attention Capture Economy

Attention is no longer just a psychological concept; it is a commodity. And like any commodity, it is extracted, refined, packaged, and sold—with profit, not wellbeing, as the ultimate metric. What distinguishes the current digital landscape is not that it demands our attention—books, lectures, and art have always done that—but that it *monetises the process of distraction itself.* In today's economic architecture, your wandering mind is not a bug; it is the product. Tech platforms have industrialised the cultivation of passivity. They are not built to inform or empower. They are optimised to *harvest the lowest-energy engagement possible,* and in doing so, they reward mental laziness at scale.

To understand the depth of this shift, one must start with the basic mechanics of platform economics. Most major digital services—from search engines and newsfeeds to streaming sites and social media—operate on an advertising-based revenue model. They do not charge users for their core functionality. Instead, they sell advertisers *access to your attention,* measured in dwell time, impressions, clicks, and behavioural data. And here lies the structural incentive: the longer you stay, the more data you emit, and the more ads you see. This incentivises platforms not to *serve your intentions,* but to *redirect them*—not to *sharpen your focus,* but to *prolong your presence.*

The most effective way to keep users present is not through high-effort engagement. It is through *low-friction, low-value content loops*—the endless scroll, the autoplay queue, the trending tab. These features are not neutral. They are precision-engineered to trigger the brain's novelty-seeking circuitry, leveraging variable rewards and intermittent reinforcement, the same mechanisms used in slot machines. The result is a digital environment in which *attention is not directed but dispersed,* scattered across stimuli designed to *capture rather than cultivate.*

This has profound consequences for cognition. When we are repeatedly trained to consume information in fragmented, shallow bursts, our capacity for sustained focus erodes. Complex tasks—like reading a dense article, sitting with ambiguity, or building an original argument—begin to feel less accessible, not because they have changed, but because our *attentional muscles have atrophied.* And yet, the system does not punish this decline. It *rewards it.* The less you resist the pull of the feed, the more valuable you become to the platform's business model. *Mental laziness is not a side effect; it is an asset.*

The attention economy, then, is not merely a market—it is a mode of governance. It reshapes how decisions are made, not only by individuals but by institutions. News organisations, for example, are increasingly structured around click-through metrics rather than editorial integrity. Political discourse is driven not by reasoned argument but by emotional virality. Even education is pulled into the current: courses must now compete with entertainment for retention, often resorting to gamification and simplification. The very tools we once relied on to elevate thinking are now subject to the same gravitational pull: *optimise for engagement, or become invisible.*

This feedback loop is reinforced by algorithmic curation. The more you engage with low-effort content, the more the system serves it to you. Over time, your feed becomes a mirror—not of your highest intentions, but of your most exploitable impulses. The algorithm does not ask what you *aspire* to know; it feeds what you will *likely not resist.* And in doing so, it subtly narrows the range of what you see, think, and care about. *The user is free to choose, but the menu is rigged.*

Consider YouTube's recommendation engine. Studies show that it accounts for over 70% of what people watch. This means that the majority of viewing decisions are not deliberate—they are *guided by predictive systems trained on past behaviour.* What gets amplified are not the most informative or challenging ideas, but the content most likely to keep you watching. This often includes outrage, sensationalism, and low-effort entertainment. The same logic applies to TikTok, where virality is determined not by social connection but by algorithmic potential: a short, dopamine-rich video that can hijack attention in three seconds or less. *Depth is the enemy of throughput.*

This model has psychological costs. It deconditions us from boredom, which has historically been the incubator of reflection, creativity, and insight. It trains us to fear silence and struggle. And it habituates us to expect stimulation without effort—*the informational equivalent of junk food*. The more we consume, the less satisfied we become, because *what we are fed does not nourish our minds—it only pacifies them*.

Philosophically, this raises urgent questions about autonomy. If our choices are shaped by systems that optimise for passivity, can we still claim those choices as our own? Autonomy is not just the ability to click; it is the ability to reflect on *why* we click. The attention economy erodes this meta-awareness. It keeps us busy but not deliberate, connected but not conscious. We become spectators of our own scrolling.

To be clear, the goal is not to demonise distraction per se. The human mind has always wandered, and leisure is not a sin. But when distraction becomes the dominant mode of engagement, and when that mode is institutionalised by billion-dollar incentive structures, the stakes change. What is at risk is not just productivity—it is *cognitive sovereignty*.

Some have argued that users can simply "choose better"—that if individuals wanted more meaningful content, they could seek it out. But this argument ignores the asymmetry of power between platform and person. Most users do not control the design of the interface, the structure of the incentives, or the logic of the algorithm. These are invisible forces that shape behaviour upstream of conscious choice. To ask individuals to resist an entire industrial complex through personal discipline alone is both unrealistic and unfair. *The problem is not individual willpower; it is systemic architecture.*

The solution, then, is not abstention, but awareness—and eventually, redesign. Platforms must be held accountable not just for *what they make possible,* but for *what they make probable.* This includes rethinking the metrics of success. Instead of measuring attention purely by volume, we must begin to measure it by *value.* What does this time spent lead to? Does it inform, challenge, expand? Or does it numb, reinforce, and regress?

There are precedents for such shifts. In food, public pressure led to clearer labelling and regulations around addictive additives. In finance, exploitative lending practices were reclassified and penalised. A similar reckoning is needed in the digital sphere. Attention is not just a market to be exploited—it is a resource to be protected. And like any scarce resource, it requires stewardship.

This stewardship will demand changes in design culture, in public policy, and in consumer expectation. Designers must learn to differentiate between engagement and exploitation. Regulators must begin to treat attention as a public good, not a private currency. And users must cultivate a new kind of literacy—not just about how platforms work, but about how *they* work when on those platforms. What pulls them in, what leaves them dull, what makes them pause.

In this sense, the attention economy is not just a challenge; it is a mirror. It reflects the cognitive values we tolerate, the mental habits we reward, and the kind of citizens we are becoming. If we want a society that values thought over reaction, intention over impulse, and truth over traffic, we cannot leave our attentional lives to chance. We must reclaim the right not just to choose what we see, but to *shape the systems that shape those choices.*

Only then can we begin to build a digital culture that does not mine attention, but *honours it.* That does not reduce us to eyeballs, but restores us as minds. That does not monetise our weakness, but reinforces our strength. Such a culture will not emerge through inertia. It will require effort, imagination, and collective will. But the alternative—an economy that thrives on our unthinking—is far more costly.

Rethinking Design for Human Strengths

Much of modern technology is not built to elevate us—it is engineered to manage us. From algorithms that guess what we want before we think to ask, to platforms that soothe every friction point in the user experience, contemporary design culture largely optimises for passivity. The ideal user, in many product ecosystems, is one who rarely questions, never pauses, and returns without being prompted. Yet in doing so, design practices risk bypassing what makes us distinctively human: our capacity for effortful cognition, nuanced judgement, and volitional choice. *The more technology does "for" us, the less it does "with" us—and the more it erodes the conditions under which agency, growth, and maturity can flourish.*

To rethink design for human strengths is not to shun innovation. It is to recover the original ambition of human-centred technology: not to pacify the user, but to partner with them. This entails a fundamental reorientation—from tools that replace human faculties to ones that reinforce them; from experiences that reduce decision-making to those that cultivate discernment. In short, it demands design that stretches the mind rather than shielding it.

The commercial logic of most interfaces today privileges stickiness and ease above all else. Consider the home screen of a modern smartphone: a theatre of instant gratification, sensory comfort, and algorithmic persuasion. Every icon is a promise of something immediate—be it entertainment, relief, or stimulation. UX principles are engineered not around enhancing reflection or learning, but around minimising "drop-off." Complexity is filtered out, challenge flattened. The interface behaves like a concierge, not a coach. *This is not accidental; it is architecture shaped by incentive.*

However, ease is not neutral. When everything flows too smoothly, the user ceases to notice the path they are taking, or even that a path is being taken at all. Psychological research has long demonstrated that friction—well-placed difficulty—can heighten attention, deepen memory, and reinforce learning. Cognitive strain, when applied judiciously, cultivates stamina and resilience. Remove all resistance, and you remove the context in which human faculties grow. In this sense, modern interface design often functions like a cognitive monoculture: streamlined, efficient, and utterly impoverished.

What would it mean, then, to design *for* human strengths? First, it requires recognising what those strengths actually are. Humans are not optimised for speed or precision—machines outperform us there. Our strengths lie elsewhere: in empathy, narrative thinking, layered understanding, ethical discernment, and creative problem-solving. These capacities thrive not in environments of endless automation but in conditions that allow for effort, ambiguity, and meaning-making. *Design that reinforces these qualities is not nostalgic—it is anticipatory.*

Take, for instance, the educational technology sector. Many digital learning platforms are designed to remove "frustration" from the student's experience. Auto-correcting algorithms, multiple-choice scaffolding, and gamified feedback loops often sidestep the messiness of real learning. But consider an alternative: a platform that intentionally introduces complexity, prompts metacognitive reflection, and rewards sustained engagement rather than instant answers. Such a tool may be less "sticky," but it would be cognitively generative. It would be built not just for engagement metrics, but for intellectual maturity.

Another example can be found in digital note-taking applications. The dominant model privileges speed and accessibility—type, tap, sync, forget. But emergent platforms like Roam Research or Obsidian take a different approach. Their design philosophy invites users to *connect* ideas, not just capture them; to revisit, revise, and recursively link concepts over time. This friction—this need to actively shape one's information landscape—does not slow cognition; it *stimulates* it. It is a subtle act of resistance against disposability and cognitive outsourcing.

There is an ethical dimension to this rethinking as well. The principle of "designing for ease" is often presented as a benevolent gesture: make life simpler, smoother, kinder. But simplicity for its own sake can infantilise. When users are shielded from effort entirely, they are also denied the opportunity to develop judgement. Just as good parenting doesn't mean removing every obstacle from a child's path, good design doesn't mean eliminating all complexity. *Sometimes, design must demand more from us—because we are capable of more.*

Contrast this with behavioural "nudge" systems now embedded in many digital environments. These systems often rely on subtle manipulations to steer users toward desired outcomes—subscribe, buy, swipe, stay. While these tactics may be effective in guiding behaviour, they bypass the very faculties they claim to serve. They presume that human rationality is a liability to be circumvented, not a strength to be engaged. This is where behavioural design and humanistic design diverge. One seeks control; the other seeks cultivation.

To be clear, friction is not inherently virtuous. Poor design that confuses or frustrates without purpose is not what is being advocated. But intentional, meaningful friction—designed as a prompt for engagement, thought, or choice—can elevate a system from convenience to relevance. Such friction reminds the user: you are not just a consumer of experience, but a co-creator of it.

The stakes of this design philosophy become even clearer when viewed through the lens of collective decision-making. Consider the interfaces we use to engage with news, politics, and public discourse. These platforms increasingly reward impulsive reactions—likes, shares, outrage—while discouraging depth, context, or deliberation. The design nudges us toward immediacy rather than wisdom. But what if these same platforms were built to reward time-on-thought, to surface counterpoints, to prompt source tracing before dissemination? These are not hypothetical features; they are design choices awaiting implementation. *The platform does not just carry the message; it shapes the mind.*

At the core of this reimagining is a simple but radical proposition: *design should challenge users because people rise to challenge.* It should not assume fragility or seek to shield users from their own capacities. Rather, it should act as a crucible for growth—an environment where effort is respected, not engineered away.

In this light, design is not merely aesthetic or functional. It becomes moral. Every interface is a set of values made visible. Are we building tools that extend human dignity and cognitive sovereignty, or are we building dependencies masked as convenience? Are we optimising for momentary pleasure or for durable capability?

To design for human strengths, then, is not to regress into analogue nostalgia. It is to design with a future-facing respect for what people *could be,* not merely what they currently demand. It is to believe that technology can be a medium for maturation, not just gratification. That belief must be built into the wireframes, the workflows, and the very assumptions of the tools we use.

When design refuses to underestimate us, we have the chance to become more.

Chapter 10
The Thinking Person's Resistance Manual

In the digital age, the most vital form of intelligence may not be computational or even creative—it may be defensive. The skill that matters most is recognising when thinking has quietly been outsourced, and taking it back. Automation promised liberation from menial tasks, a release of mental bandwidth. Instead, what often arrives is subtler: a gradual atrophy of thought, disguised as convenience. When an app dictates your route, your playlist, your memory, your responses, your purchases, or even your attention, what remains of genuine volition? Mental independence now demands active upkeep; it cannot be inherited passively.

This is not an argument against technology. It is a call to resist its misuse through deliberate cognition. When platforms exploit impulse, reward speed, and dull discomfort, the countermeasure is internal: cultivating awareness so that reflection—not automation—governs your mind.

The slide into outsourced thinking begins subtly. Autocomplete finishes sentences; recommendation engines shape taste; algorithmic curation displaces judgment. These tools are not intrinsically harmful. Yet when used unconsciously, they establish a pattern: thinking becomes something delegated rather than assumed. Like unused muscles, the faculties of memory, attention, and reflection atrophy—not because of resistance, but from neglect.

This is the quiet crisis of our time: cognitive complacency masquerading as efficiency. And it will not resolve itself. Just as physical fitness requires active conditioning in a world designed for sedentariness, mental sovereignty demands effort within an environment optimised for passivity. Resistance is not instinctive—it must be cultivated.

It begins with recognition: the ability to detect when your mind is being managed for you. This is the first discipline of cognitive self-defence. Distinguishing between using a tool and being used by it is both a moral and mental frontier. When presented with a default option, question whether it aligns with your values or merely your habits. When a prompt appears, ask whether it serves thought or interrupts it. To reclaim the right to think is to pause where speed is demanded, to slow down where momentum is assumed.

Awareness alone is insufficient. Cognitive strength is rebuilt through intentional friction—not as punishment, but as provocation. A life without challenge is a mind without stimulus. Practices that complicate the immediate—writing by hand, recalling from memory, debating without notes, pausing before responding—restore the neural texture that complexity requires. Friction is not an enemy of design; it is the condition for thoughtfulness.

The marketplace offers no incentive for this. Silicon Valley prizes scale, not sovereignty. Platforms optimise for retention, not resilience. Business models monetise attention; distraction is currency. In such an ecosystem, personal responsibility becomes radical. This is not about digital detoxes or Luddite retreats—it is about reshaping habits, environments, and mental postures.

To that end, mental strength training must become a living practice. Not vague affirmations, but tangible disciplines to rebuild thought's architecture. Memory exercises that stretch retrieval, attention drills that resist fragmentation, decision protocols that restore deliberation. These are not productivity hacks or therapy tools—they are civic instruments. Just as free societies rely on informed citizens, free minds depend on exercised faculties.

The test is found in daily choices: reaching for your phone in silence, accepting the first search result without scrutiny, multitasking out of boredom rather than necessity. Micro-moments accumulate, shaping cognitive identity. Are you someone who reacts or reflects? Seeks stimulation or generates it? Offloads difficulty or carries it thoughtfully? Each decision votes for your long-term mental condition.

Agency requires stewardship of your own cognition. This means designing at the level of daily practice, not just apps and workflows. Mundane interventions—morning rituals for clarity, workspace constraints that limit interruptions, deliberate reading habits resisting skimming—are acts of sovereignty. Each declares: I will not be programmed. I will not be streamlined into docility.

Agency is not a switch; it is a muscle. Like all muscles, it strengthens under strain, not sedation. In a culture that prizes ease, difficulty must be courted. In an economy built on habit, patterns must be broken. In interfaces designed for passivity, participation must be insisted upon. This chapter offers no silver bullets—only habits, questions, systems, and provocations. A manual of resistance not because you are besieged, but because your mind is too valuable to leave undefended.

The thinking person's resistance is quiet. It is not loud, angry, or performative. It is a vigilant posture: refusing to surrender attention, memory, and deliberation to indifferent machines. The future belongs not to those who outsource their minds, but to those who shape them—deliberately, daily, and with unshakable respect for the capacity to choose.

Cognitive Self-Defence

There is a quiet substitution taking place—so seamless that most people never notice. One moment, you're deciding how to respond to a message; the next, predictive text completes the thought for you. One minute, you're seeking information; the next, an algorithm curates what it believes you want. These aren't conveniences so much as incursions—subtle appropriations of cognitive effort dressed in the language of efficiency. What was once an act of conscious deliberation has become, almost imperceptibly, a reflexive tap, swipe, or scroll. *Cognitive self-defence begins with the recognition that not all help is harmless—and not all friction is failure.*

The defining feature of many contemporary digital tools is that they do the thinking for us. But thought is not something to be efficiently bypassed. It is the scaffolding of autonomy. The erosion of effort in decision-making, memory, and problem-solving is not a technical inevitability; it is a design choice. And this choice is rarely neutral. Behind every "smart" feature—every autofill, algorithmic suggestion, and push notification—is a commercial interest that benefits from minimising your cognitive resistance. The less you pause, the more you click. The more you rely, the more predictable you become. *Dependence is not a side-effect—it is the product.*

To defend one's cognitive autonomy is not to reject technology, but to use it consciously, critically, and with clarity about its intentions. This requires a new mental posture: one that resists the passive posture of digital drift and embraces active discernment. Just as physical self-defence begins with situational awareness, cognitive self-defence starts with the ability to notice when your thinking is being intercepted. When a platform structures your choices, ask: what assumptions are being baked into this design? When a shortcut is offered, ask: what am I being disincentivised from doing on my own?

A classic example is GPS navigation. Useful? Undeniably. But repeated reliance without intentional counterbalance leads to *wayfinding atrophy*—the brain's spatial orientation and memory functions degrade when outsourced. In 2006, researchers at University College London found that the hippocampus—the region associated with spatial navigation—was measurably more developed in London taxi drivers who navigated from memory than in those who relied on digital aids. The tool didn't just change their routes—it changed their brains. The principle extends beyond geography. *Every act of offloading a mental task, if done habitually and uncritically, weakens the corresponding cognitive muscle.*

Recognition must be followed by recalibration. This means reinstating habits that require mental effort—not because they are harder, but because they make you more cognitively sovereign. Write down what you want to remember rather than relying on a search engine to store and retrieve it. Delay responses in digital conversations to allow time for reflection rather than defaulting to rapid-fire replies. Choose longform reading over snippets. These aren't nostalgic gestures; they are neurological training. *Friction, when intentional, is a form of fortification.*

Defence also involves environment design. Just as nutritional self-discipline depends on what's in the fridge, cognitive discipline depends on what surrounds your attention. Disable default notifications. Structure digital spaces to reduce passive exposure—hide auto-playing feeds, unsubscribe from unfiltered updates, switch devices to greyscale if colour stimuli prove compulsive. These aren't acts of restriction; they're acts of alignment. You're tuning your environment to support agency, not undermine it. *The real battle for your mind is fought in moments that seem too small to matter—and repeated until they do.*

But awareness and environment alone are not enough. At the core of cognitive self-defence lies a deeper discipline: *reclaiming the right to be uncertain*. Much of what we offload to technology is discomfort—ambiguity, delay, difficulty. The cost is fluency in ambiguity itself, which is essential for ethical reflection, complex problem-solving, and intellectual growth. Resist the impulse to resolve uncertainty with immediate Googling. Sit with the question. Let it mature in your mind. *To not know immediately is not a failure—it's a space for thought to breathe.*

Technology's seduction lies in its ease. But ease is not always a virtue. When digital design removes all resistance, it removes the very conditions under which deep thinking thrives. Consider autocomplete in writing. What seems like a time-saver subtly reshapes the language you use, nudging you toward predictable phrasing. Over time, this influences your mental lexicon. The cost is not just originality—it's ownership. Are you writing, or are you editing a machine's suggestion? *Cognitive self-defence means reclaiming authorship at the level of thought, not just output.*

None of this implies ascetic withdrawal from the digital world. It demands engagement with discernment. A surgeon uses tools with precision, not dependency. Similarly, we must learn to use digital systems as instruments of augmentation, not replacement. That begins by asking, again and again: is this tool making me sharper or duller? More discerning or more automated? Is this task worth doing with effort because the effort matters?

There is a quiet power in deliberate resistance. Not dramatic gestures, but small, persistent acts of mental presence. When you choose to recall a fact instead of searching it, when you write an email without a template, when you take time to form your own view rather than echo a trending opinion—you are *practising autonomy in a culture designed for delegation*. You are asserting that thought is not a liability to be optimised away, but a discipline to be defended.

The most dangerous erosion is not of knowledge, but of *mental posture*: the readiness to think before reacting, to ask before accepting, to wonder before concluding. The core strategy of cognitive self-defence is not merely to protect attention or memory, but to preserve *the will to think in the first place*. That will, once surrendered, is difficult to recover. But it can be rebuilt—patiently, deliberately, and with tools you already possess.

Cognitive self-defence is not a task to complete; it is a way of being to inhabit. It is less about resisting machines than refusing to become machine-like. In an age of engineered ease, the thinking person must train not for speed, but for *sovereignty*. The mind, after all, is not a node to be managed—it is a territory to be defended. And the smallest gesture of effort—when chosen consciously—becomes a border wall against encroaching automation.

Reintroducing Intentional Friction

The default logic of contemporary technology is seamlessness. Everything must be smooth, fast, and automatic—frictionless by design. We order meals with a tap, unlock our phones with a glance, answer emails with predictive phrases. If we must think, even briefly, the system is considered broken. The goal, it seems, is to eliminate hesitation, delay, and ambiguity—not merely as inefficiencies, but as intolerable obstructions. Yet *what if those very obstructions are where our minds do their most essential work?* What if friction is not a failure of design, but its forgotten virtue?

Intentional friction is not about inefficiency for its own sake; it is about *reclaiming moments that make thinking unavoidable*. Deliberate delay, required recall, or optional complexity are not nuisances—they are training grounds for agency, reflection, and mastery. In systems where everything is made easy, we grow cognitively inert. In contrast, when systems are designed to *challenge rather than pacify*, the user is compelled to engage—actively, attentively, and on their own terms. *Ease without engagement is not progress. It is the quiet erosion of participation.*

Consider the humble map. Paper maps required spatial reasoning, path planning, and a working knowledge of terrain. Digital navigation apps have replaced those demands with real-time voice guidance and rerouting. The result? Fewer navigational errors—and fewer opportunities to build internal representations of space. In 2017, a study published in *Nature Communications* showed that individuals using GPS for prolonged periods had *measurable reductions in hippocampal activation*. The map didn't just remove friction—it removed the mental work. *And when the mind stops working, it stops growing.*

This principle applies well beyond travel. When you receive recommended content based on your viewing history, you're less likely to search actively, evaluate critically, or explore widely. When platforms autoplay the next video or scroll infinitely, you don't decide to continue—you merely fail to opt out. These features are not accidental; they are *friction-reducing mechanisms designed to bypass deliberate choice*. Their success is measured not by user benefit, but by behavioural metrics: time-on-site, click-through rates, and daily active users. The user experience is not designed for the user's growth—it's designed for the system's stickiness.

But what happens when we intentionally reinsert friction—not as punishment, but as provocation? Reintroducing intentional friction means building tools and habits that *require* participation. Not mindless repetition, but thoughtful investment. It means choosing practices that *demand effort because effort deepens comprehension, memory, and independence*. One such tool is spaced repetition: a system used in language learning and medical training that deliberately delays exposure to reinforce retention. By making you wait—by requiring you to *recall rather than reread*—spaced repetition turns memory into a mental discipline. This is friction as pedagogical strategy, not performance bottleneck.

Another example is the handwritten journal. Writing longhand slows thought, but in doing so, it forces clarity. Typing allows speed; handwriting demands synthesis. Research from Princeton University found that students who took notes by hand *remembered more and understood better* than those who typed. The additional effort created a deeper cognitive imprint. The slowing down was not a flaw—it was the source of learning. *The friction became the function.*

Technological friction is often viewed through a lens of accessibility and user-friendliness. But a different ethic is possible—*one that values cognitive challenge as a feature rather than a bug*. For instance, consider a reading app that disables scrolling and presents one paragraph at a time, requiring a swipe or tap to proceed. The design might seem cumbersome compared to continuous scroll, but it reinforces attentiveness. It cues the reader to pause, process, and progress *intentionally*. Or imagine a writing tool that disables autocorrect and predictive text, compelling users to rely on their own lexical memory and grammatical judgment. The result would not be frictionless productivity, but *cognitive re-engagement* with language itself.

Such tools are rare because they do not conform to the dominant metrics of tech valuation. Investors and executives reward scale, speed, and stickiness—not user sovereignty. Yet from an ethical design perspective, this is precisely where change must begin. Systems that value the user's mind *must build in mechanisms that preserve the need for effort*. These include confirmatory prompts that require reflection before submission, limits on algorithmic recommendations, and learning platforms that avoid over-simplification. Good friction makes us pause. And *in the pause, thinking begins.*

Intentional friction also applies at the level of social systems. The ability to think critically in digital spaces is often impaired by the absence of cognitive roadblocks. Share buttons make reposting easier than reflecting. Comment threads reward speed over thoughtfulness. Virality thrives on immediate reaction. One potential intervention is to introduce *delays by design*—mechanisms that interrupt impulsivity and incentivise deliberation. Twitter, for instance, has experimented with prompting users to *read an article before sharing it*. Such nudges act as friction that defends against mindless propagation. *Not every action deserves to be frictionless—especially when the stakes are epistemic.*

In our daily lives, we can build intentional friction into our own routines as a form of cognitive hygiene. Reading longform instead of summaries. Turning off autocomplete in digital writing. Scheduling time to think before responding. Even setting our phones to grayscale or turning off notifications during reading hours can become acts of architectural resistance—*rearranging our environments to reintroduce effort where effort matters*. These are not lifestyle hacks. They are *ethical commitments to being present inside our own thinking*.

There will always be a market for convenience. But if we continue optimising away every point of difficulty, we will find ourselves surrounded by systems that think *for* us, not *with* us. And the cost will be invisible until it is irretrievable: the gradual dulling of the very capacities we most value—curiosity, memory, discernment, judgment. The antidote is not Luddite nostalgia. It is *deliberate design that asks more of us—not less.*

Reintroducing intentional friction is a philosophical act disguised as a practical one. It affirms that human thought is worth the trouble, that struggle is often a signal of something real happening in the mind. We do not learn by bypassing challenge—we learn by *engaging with it*. In a culture of shortcuts, detours become discipline. Slowness becomes sovereignty. Discomfort becomes depth.

Friction is not the enemy of progress. It is the scaffolding of understanding. And as we redesign our digital environments and personal habits, we must ask: what if the very effort we seek to avoid is the very effort that defines us as thinking beings? *Friction reminds us we are still participating. Friction, thoughtfully chosen, is how we remember we are still human.*

Mental Strength Training

One of the most overlooked truths of the modern cognitive landscape is that mental strength—like physical strength—does not emerge from intention alone. It is the product of repeated effort against resistance. Yet in a culture increasingly optimised for ease, our inner faculties are not only underutilised; they are actively atrophied. Platforms anticipate our choices, devices remind us before we forget, and algorithms buffer us from ambiguity. The result is a form of cognitive domestication—mental agility dulled by frictionless convenience. In this context, rebuilding memory, attention, and decision-making power is not a return to the past, but an act of necessary adaptation. *Mental fitness is no longer a given; it must be trained for deliberately, just as a sedentary person must train to walk uphill again.*

This training begins with recognising that mental strength cannot be abstract. It emerges from *practice,* not promise. Take memory, for instance. What was once considered a defining element of intelligence is now outsourced to digital prosthetics. Birthdays, directions, facts, appointments—all live elsewhere. While some view this as benign delegation, cognitive science disagrees. The act of remembering—of effortfully retrieving information—strengthens synaptic patterns and neural pathways. The absence of such effort, over time, leads to structural decline. Studies from neuropsychology reveal that memory consolidation depends not simply on exposure, but on active engagement: recalling, connecting, and rehearsing. Therefore, rebuilding memory strength must start by reintroducing recall as a regular activity. Commit a poem to memory. Retain phone numbers by choice. Remove the autocomplete function from frequently used apps and force the brain to re-engage. *The memory muscle does not grow when information is merely available; it grows when information is earned.*

The same logic applies to attention. We speak of attention as if it were a passive possession—something we either have or don't. But attention is better understood as *an active skill,* shaped by environment, honed through discipline, and susceptible to erosion. Most digital environments fragment this skill by design, turning it into a commodity rather than a capacity. Notifications, infinite scrolls, and multitasking norms breed a state of permanent partial focus. To reverse this, attention must be reconditioned through sustained effort. Begin with controlled abstention: set a timer for uninterrupted reading. Turn off all alerts during focused work. Practice mono-tasking in defiance of the multitasking myth. Crucially, reward comes not from duration alone, but from the quality of engagement. Meditative attentional drills, such as candle-gazing or timed observation of a single image, can be surprisingly effective. Cognitive behavioural protocols suggest that *even ten minutes a day of sustained attention exercises can reshape attentional thresholds over time.*

Decision-making, perhaps the most executive of our mental faculties, also suffers from disuse. In an interface culture where most choices are pre-sorted, pre-selected, or defaulted, the act of weighing options is increasingly rare. Recommendation engines choose our entertainment. Filters pre-empt our searches. Autoplay dictates our next move. But decision-making, like any high-order cognition, thrives on deliberation. It involves trade-offs, values, consequence modelling—all of which require cognitive energy. To build strength here, one must *deliberately take back the burden of choice.* Resist default settings. Try ordering food without relying on past orders or reviews. Construct personal frameworks for making hard decisions—one useful method being the "reversal test" (asking whether the opposite of a proposed change would seem equally appealing or problematic). Another is "value-mapping," where decisions are ranked not by outcome but by alignment with long-term goals. The mental effort this demands is not a flaw; it is a feature. *The goal is not to make life harder, but to keep the decision-making apparatus intact and agile.*

Across all these domains, what unites memory, attention, and decision-making is the requirement of *deliberate friction*. This friction is not punitive. It is, in fact, pedagogical. When we add a few extra seconds to a task—pausing before responding, recalling rather than searching, considering rather than swiping—we are not just slowing down; we are reclaiming territory ceded to convenience. Each moment of effort is a quiet protest against passive cognition. Over time, these moments accumulate into habits, and those habits coalesce into mental character.

There are powerful historical echoes here. The ancient Stoics practised "voluntary discomfort" to train resilience. The medieval monastics engaged in repetition and memorisation as forms of spiritual discipline. Even in recent decades, elite performers across fields have embraced mental conditioning routines that resemble cognitive strength training: chess masters studying endgames in silence, pilots rehearsing procedures blindfolded, musicians memorising symphonies note-for-note. The pattern is clear: *when the stakes are high, thinking is treated as a skill to be honed—not a process to be outsourced.*

Today's stakes are no lower. In fact, they may be higher. In an environment where mental ease is engineered, the capacity to engage in effortful thought becomes a form of autonomy. But this autonomy is fragile. It must be cultivated through daily, deliberate practice—practices that make thought effortful again, not for nostalgia's sake, but because *clarity, judgement, and resilience depend on it*. Whether one chooses journaling over tweeting, discussion over commenting, or reading over summarising, the underlying principle is the same: *choose the path that demands something of your mind.*

Mental strength is not an aesthetic ideal. It is a survival trait. And like all traits forged in resistance, it is not built by what is easy—it is built by what is earned.

Everyday Practices of Cognitive Ownership

No one wakes up one morning to find their thinking outsourced. It happens gradually—one shortcut, one passive scroll, one auto-filled answer at a time. Cognitive decline in the age of smart technology is rarely dramatic. It is, instead, an erosion: *a subtle evacuation of agency from the inside out*. And what makes this erosion dangerous is precisely what makes it invisible—it disguises itself as efficiency. In such a climate, *cognitive ownership is not simply a virtue; it is a discipline*. The most powerful resistance does not come from grand gestures, but from the accumulated force of small, deliberate acts: routines that reclaim control, rituals that restore depth, decisions that reassert authorship over the mind's activity.

Owning one's cognition begins with how we structure time. One of the most quietly subversive acts a person can perform today is to begin the day without a screen. Those first minutes after waking represent a neurological sweet spot—where memory consolidation, attentional readiness, and emotional tone are most pliable. When this space is immediately filled with newsfeeds, alerts, and algorithmic content, we surrender the architecture of thought to someone else's priorities. But individuals who begin their mornings with analogue rituals—journaling, slow reading, walking in silence—often report a qualitatively different mental state across the rest of the day. These are not sentimental habits; they are strategic. *They reintroduce pacing, reflection, and interiority into a culture obsessed with instant reaction.*

This is not merely anecdotal. Psychological studies in attentional drift, including work from Harvard's psychology lab, demonstrate that fragmented attention in the first 30 minutes of the day sets a lower attentional baseline for the next four hours. In contrast, subjects who engaged in single-task activities early in the morning—especially tasks requiring memory or planning—maintained significantly higher cognitive control throughout the day. The implications are clear: *what begins as a private routine rapidly becomes a public asset—greater discernment, improved communication, and stronger resistance to distraction.*

Another pillar of cognitive ownership is intentional language use. When we uncritically adopt the linguistic frames handed to us by apps and interfaces—such as "likes," "followers," "engagement," or "trending"—we not only speak differently, we begin to think differently. Language is not neutral. It encodes assumptions, expectations, and values. For example, describing online interactions as "engagement" implies reciprocity, when many are actually asymmetrical or performative. Calling a video "viral" suggests natural appeal, when it may be the product of algorithmic amplification. Thoughtful users interrupt this drift by choosing words deliberately. They speak of "attention currency" rather than "time online," or "algorithmic selection" rather than "personalised content." *This linguistic precision reasserts clarity in a domain engineered for blurring.*

Equally transformative is the practice of slow decision-making. We are conditioned to believe that hesitation signals weakness or confusion, but in cognitive terms, *deliberation is often the highest form of mental clarity*. The speed at which apps demand decisions—swipe left, click buy, skip ad—trains us in reflex rather than reason. But when individuals reintroduce pauses into daily decision flows, they restore cognitive autonomy. This can take the form of simple interventions: setting a 60-second delay before any online purchase, writing down three reasons for or against a choice before clicking "yes," or physically stepping away from a screen before replying to a heated message. These are not quirks of temperament; they are tools of ownership. They create room for second-order thinking: *not just what am I choosing, but who is choosing within me*?

Reflection, too, is an everyday tool of cognitive ownership, especially when structured. Unstructured rumination often masquerades as reflection but tends to reinforce emotional bias or habitual narratives. Structured reflection, by contrast, offers the scaffolding for insight. One effective format is the "three-layer" reflection method: first, describe an event; second, analyse the internal reaction; third, reframe the significance. This form is used in elite military debriefs, therapeutic protocols, and leadership coaching. A similar method used in cognitive behavioural therapy—the "ABC model" (Activating event, Beliefs, Consequences)—has been shown to *reduce impulsive behaviour and improve decision-making coherence over time*.

In addition to reflective writing, many professionals build "cognitive audit" rituals into their week. These typically involve asking: What did I think well about this week? What did I outsource that I should have owned? Where did I fall into passivity? These are not self-flagellating exercises. They are acts of recalibration. Without regular audits, the mind is vulnerable to drift—toward comfort, mimicry, or over-reliance on systems that think for us.

Importantly, these practices are not limited to the private sphere. Ownership scales. In group settings—teams, classrooms, families—collective cognitive habits shape shared norms. Some teams begin meetings with "pre-thoughts," where each member writes down initial responses to a prompt before discussion begins, to avoid groupthink. Others use analogue tools—whiteboards, post-it frameworks—to decentralise digital dependencies. In classrooms, "thinking journals" are re-emerging, not as grading instruments but as meta-cognitive spaces where students reflect not just on what they learned, but how they approached the learning itself. These methods are grounded in a simple truth: *thinking improves when thinking is visible.*

Real-world examples offer compelling evidence. At a media company in Berlin, executives banned internal emails on Fridays and replaced them with face-to-face problem-solving sessions. Their aim was not nostalgia, but focus—forcing teams to engage with complexity, nuance, and unpredictability without digital crutches. Over a six-month period, creativity scores and project completion times both improved. In Tokyo, a software firm redesigned its workflow to include "cognitive breaks"—scheduled pauses for non-digital activity such as reading or drawing. Employees reported higher energy and lower error rates. These are not accidental benefits; they are designed results, born from environments that value mental presence over interface fluency.

Cognitive ownership is not about rejecting technology. It is about *choosing the terms on which we engage with it*. Tools can amplify intelligence, but only if they are used from a position of authorship rather than surrender. Each practice outlined above—morning routines, precise language, slow decisions, structured reflection, team rituals—acts as a counterweight to ambient automation. They remind the mind that it is still the pilot, not just the passenger.

At its core, cognitive ownership is a question of dignity. In a world eager to think for us, every act of self-generated thought—every pause, every reflection, every question asked before answering—is a quiet but powerful claim: *my mind is mine*. And from that claim arises not just clarity, but strength. Not just independence, but discernment. Not just resistance, but renewal.

Chapter 11
Thought, Reclaimed

The most persistent illusion of contemporary technology is not that it frees us, but that it thinks for us at no cost. We swipe, speak, and scroll through decisions, believing ourselves empowered, while the faculties that once defined human intelligence—attention, memory, deliberate reasoning—slowly atrophy in the background. This book has done more than critique smart devices as mere distractions or enablers of dependency. It has traced a deeper, more unsettling reality: that we are active participants in the outsourcing of thought. To reclaim thinking is not to reject technology, but to reassert the mind's sovereignty. It is to cultivate a life in which cognition is foundational, not incidental.

What would such a life entail? Not in abstraction, but in daily, intentional practice? How might we design existence not around mere convenience or accessibility, but around cognitive integrity? This chapter serves as both synthesis and culmination of preceding insights. Earlier sections dissected manipulative design, interrogated the ethics of ease, and proposed strategies for mental resistance; here, the emphasis shifts to constructive architecture. The pressing question is no longer what technology does to us, but what we are prepared to do differently.

Reclaiming thought requires a conscious reckoning with cognitive cost—a mental ledger of attention, friction, and agency. Every interface we engage with either diminishes or strengthens our capacity to think. Most default features—autoplay, predictive text, push notifications—exist not to serve your intellect but to maximise engagement, foster passive absorption, and encourage dependency masquerading as convenience. The person who reclaims mental sovereignty understands this economic model intimately, not as a distant critic, but as an active participant. They ask at every turn: does this tool cultivate my mind, or substitute for it?

This deceptively simple question forms the pivot of the chapter. The goal is not Luddite withdrawal, nor superficial "digital detoxes" that patch symptoms without addressing the underlying patterns of disengagement. It is the construction of a sustainable framework—a mode of seeing, selecting, and shaping one's environment with cognitive dignity at its core. Values must shift. In a society conditioned to prize frictionless experience, difficulty must be rehabilitated as meaningful. Not all effort is suffering; not all delay is inefficiency. Many of the richest human gains—learning, reflection, discernment—demand what modern systems strive to eliminate: pause, ambiguity, contradiction, and the slow accrual of time.

This is not a call to romanticise pre-digital life. It is, rather, an invitation to develop what might be termed techno-discernment: the skill of evaluating every digital encounter not by ease or novelty, but by its effect on the scaffolding of thought. Does it train attention or scatter it? Does it reward memory or render it unnecessary? Does it compel decision-making or make the decision for you? These are not philosophical luxuries—they are survival questions in a world of ambient computation, where intelligence is embedded in thermostats, glasses, cars, and toothbrushes.

Consider calendars. A default system auto-populates events, suggests appointments, and reminds you when to leave. Yet a person designing for thought might construct a calendar manually, reviewing commitments and adding entries by hand. This is not inefficiency—it is strategy. It introduces cognitive friction precisely where it matters: in the allocation of attention and time. Similarly, scheduled "pull" moments replace constant push notifications, offering unbroken spans of cognitive continuity, rare and immensely valuable.

Spatial design also matters. Smart speakers offer convenience—voice-activated reminders, music, instant queries—but in doing so, they flatten deliberation. By contrast, bookshelves, notepads, analogue timers, and whiteboards demand engagement. They provoke thinking rather than performing it. Those who structure their surroundings for reflection, rather than reaction, report higher creativity, reduced fatigue, and improved memory retention.

Time itself is a terrain to be curated. Cognitive sovereignty requires resisting default schedules imposed by others, identifying peak thinking hours, and guarding them for deep work. Constant availability is often the enemy of originality. Protecting periods that produce no immediate output is not indulgence—it is the foundation of intellectual productivity, built upon absorption, synthesis, and silence.

Reclaiming thought extends to the social sphere. Cognitive health is not merely personal; it is relational. Conversations that reinforce agency—through dialectical questioning, shared reflection, and patience—nourish the mind. By contrast, networks optimised for speed and performativity—comment threads, direct messages, group chats—reward shallow engagement. Those designing for mental resilience write long letters, ask genuine questions, tolerate conversational pauses, and favour interlocutors who challenge rather than echo. Language itself is formative; to fragment expression is to fragment thought.

A life centred on thinking is not constant exertion nor monastic withdrawal. It is a rhythm: alternating effort and recovery, silence and dialogue, absorption and expression. The mind, like the body, thrives on intentional tension. Strength requires weight. That weight comes in forms such as demanding books, handwritten notes, long unaccompanied walks, and conversations without agendas. These are not luxuries—they are modern necessities, resisting the gravity of passive consumption.

This chapter offers more than summary or exhortation. It presents a practical orientation to life after awareness—a life designed not for convenience, but for deliberate cognitive cultivation. It equips readers with a lens to evaluate any future interface, app, or device not merely by features, but by its impact on thinking architecture. This lens may be the book's most enduring contribution. The goal is not simply to think more, but to live as someone who preserves the conditions for thinking—and, in doing so, to construct a life of lasting intelligence rather than transient efficiency.

Designing a Mind-Conscious Life

To live intelligently in the age of smart technology is no longer about access to information, but the cultivation of discernment—*a steady capacity to choose when and how to think, rather than be thought for*. This subtle but foundational shift defines the mind-conscious life: not a life of avoidance or resistance, but of design. It is not about abstaining from tech, but about reengineering our relationship to it. In this context, every digital interaction becomes a site of decision—not just *what* we use, but *how* it shapes our inner landscape: attention, memory, agency, and self-direction. The tools have become ambient. Therefore, so must our awareness.

A life built on thoughtfulness does not emerge by default. It must be *architected*. And the materials of that architecture are not technological in origin—they are cognitive. What we centre, what we repeat, what we reward, what we allow frictionless—all these habits become infrastructure. The modern human being is not merely surrounded by interfaces—they are *shaped* by them. The most consequential effects of technology are not always visible in the moment of use. They appear over time, as patterns of unthinking accumulate into personality traits. Passive navigation becomes our cognitive signature. This is why *the most valuable metric in digital life is not speed, convenience, or output—but cognitive cost.*

Cognitive cost is not the same as effort. It is the *unseen tax on our mental resources*—the attention we forfeit to interruptions, the memory we outsource to devices, the decision-making we cede to algorithms. To become fluent in this economy is to stop asking, "What does this app do for me?" and begin asking, "What does it do to the way I think?" It is to realise that technologies once framed as time-saving often generate a long-term deficit of depth. A voice assistant that anticipates needs may feel helpful, but when used habitually, it erodes situational recall, dulls planning skills, and shifts problem-solving from a lived process to a transaction. This is not neutral. It is transformation, disguised as assistance.

Living a mind-conscious life begins with shifting one's internal value system away from comfort and toward cognitive integrity. That shift is neither ascetic nor punitive. It simply restores what has been obscured: the understanding that mental strain, when rightly applied, is the source of *clarity*, not fatigue. The friction we've been trained to eliminate—pausing before responding, recalling before searching, drafting before posting—is often the very soil in which original thought takes root. The mind-conscious person seeks not to make life harder, but to make it *meaningful through engagement*.

Consider the principle of *intentional friction* in decision-making. Most consumer interfaces are designed to flatten thought. Buy-now buttons, default settings, infinite scroll—all minimise pause. Yet these same design affordances often strip away the very moment in which human agency lives: the second of deliberation, the interval of reconsideration, the reflective gap. A mind-conscious life reclaims those milliseconds. It reinstates prompts—tools, practices, and routines that introduce pause where default systems remove it. This might take the form of disabling one-click ordering, using paper-based to-do lists, or reviewing the day ahead each morning without screens. These aren't nostalgic affectations. *They are deliberate scaffolds to protect attention as a finite resource.*

Designing for attention means making it visible. Attention is not just what we give, but what we *are given to*. If our environment is saturated with dopamine loops—notifications, autoplay feeds, artificially urgent tasks—then what we experience as desire is often only design echoing back to us. A mind-conscious life does not eliminate desire. It questions its origin. Why am I opening this app? What was I doing before? What will I be doing after? These are not spiritual questions. They are *executive function checks*. To ask them regularly is to resynchronise attention with intention.

This mindset extends to memory. In the age of ambient reminders and digital recall, *remembering becomes a radical act*. We no longer *have* to remember, but we forget at a cost.

Cognitive science is unequivocal: memory is not just storage—it is *structure*. It influences perception, fuels creativity, strengthens reasoning, and builds identity. When we offload it reflexively, we weaken not just recollection, but reasoning. A life designed for memory resists default outsourcing. It might involve handwritten journaling, spaced repetition systems, or simply choosing to recall information before retrieving it. The point is not to become a human database—it is to preserve the neural pathways that undergird thought itself.

Agency is the final pillar, and perhaps the most endangered. A well-designed tool should *extend* human agency—not mask it, displace it, or monetise it. Yet most smart technology today conflates agency with automation. A platform that decides which route you take, which news you read, or which playlist you hear has not simplified life—it has *pre-decided it*. Over time, such pre-decisioning reshapes the user into a spectator of their own routines. A life conscious of this trend does not reject automation wholesale. Instead, it applies it with criteria: does this tool *help me act*, or does it *act for me*? The difference lies in whether the human being remains a node of initiation or merely a node of confirmation.

To operationalise these principles, we must adopt a framework that is simple, portable, and rooted in practice. One model is to audit all technological engagements through four lenses: *Does this require my memory? Does this train my attention? Does this depend on my judgement? Does this reinforce my agency?* If the answer to all four is no, we are not engaging with a tool—we are being processed by one. Such auditing need not be exhaustive or moralistic. It need only be *habitual*. With repetition, it becomes second nature, forming a new layer of cognitive hygiene as essential as diet or sleep.

This same framework can be applied socially and institutionally. Educators can ask: does this learning platform encourage recall and reasoning, or reduce learning to content delivery? Managers can ask: do our workplace tools enhance focused work or fragment it with constant messaging? Designers can ask: are we building systems that reward mental shortcuts or mental strength? Every domain touched by technology is now also responsible for shaping thought. Those who design for others must learn to design *with* thought, not just around it.

Of course, perfection is neither possible nor necessary. A mind-conscious life is not one of ascetic purity or technological monogamy. It is a life of *alignment*—where our tools serve our thinking rather than shape it unconsciously. There will be trade-offs. At times, convenience will win. But the difference is that the *decision* was made, not defaulted. This is the crux. Thoughtfulness begins not in grand gestures, but in small, consistent acts of recognition.

There are examples of this lived philosophy emerging quietly, often far from Silicon Valley. A parent who reads aloud to their child nightly, not for performance but for connection. A writer who drafts essays longhand, not out of nostalgia but to honour the pace of thought. A student who sets timers for internet use, not to restrict themselves, but to protect the sanctity of mental immersion. These are not Luddites. They are designers of their own mental environments—individuals who have recognised that to think well is to live well, and that such living requires intention, not just access.

As we look forward, the future will not be defined solely by the next device, the next feature, the next wave of automation. It will be shaped by *how we think about thinking*. Whether we treat it as sacred or optional, as core or supplementary. The mind-conscious life is a blueprint—not for perfection, but for presence. It calls us not to abandon the digital world, but to inhabit it fully, with eyes open and faculties intact. It demands that we see each moment of engagement not just as a transaction of time, but as an investment in cognition.

Because in the end, the most important interface is not the screen—it is the mind that looks through it. And whether that mind remains sharp, attentive, and free is no longer a technological question. It is a design decision. Our design.

About the Author

Rowan Hale writes at the intersection of modern technology and the human mind, exploring how invisible systems reshape the way we live, think, and decide. With a background in behavioral observation and a lifelong interest in the mechanics of cognition, Hale focuses on how our environments—especially digital ones—sculpt mental habits over time. His work is driven by a deep curiosity about what we trade in exchange for convenience, and how subtle design decisions can lead to profound personal consequences. Known for his clear-eyed analysis and grounded voice, Hale helps readers reconnect with their own agency in an age of ambient automation. Why We Stop Thinking continues his mission to make the hidden architecture of everyday life visible, urgent, and debatable.

www.ingramcontent.com/pod-product-compliance
Lightning Source LLC
Chambersburg PA
CBHW031339230926
51848CB00002B/300
9789371771917